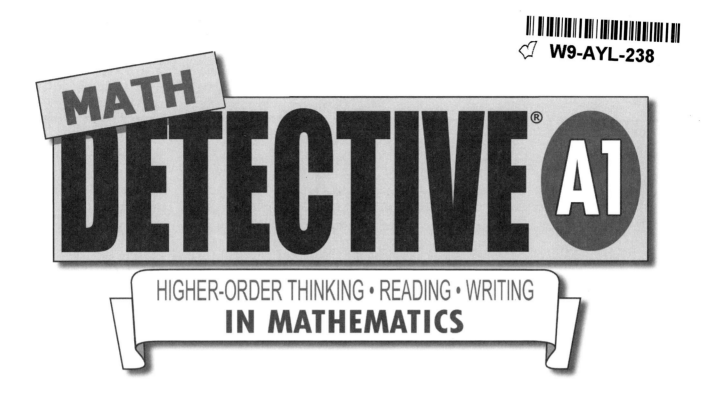

MATH DETECTIVE® A1

HIGHER-ORDER THINKING • READING • WRITING
IN MATHEMATICS

SERIES TITLES

Math Detective® Beginning, A1, B1

Reading Detective® Beginning, A1, B1

Science Detective® Beginning, A1

Terri Husted

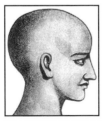

© 2003
THE CRITICAL THINKING CO.™
www.CriticalThinking.com
Phone: 800-458-4849 • Fax: 831-393-3277
P.O. Box 1610 • Seaside • CA 93955-1610
ISBN 978-0-89455-803-0

Mixed Sources
Product group from well-managed
forests and other controlled sources
www.fsc.org Cert no. SW-COC-002283
© 1996 Forest Stewardship Council

TABLE OF CONTENTS

What is *Math Detective*®?

Introduction

The problems in this book will improve your students' skills in mathematics, critical thinking, reading, and writing. The topics and skills covered are drawn from the national standards for mathematics for Grades 5-6 as outlined by the National Council of Teachers of Mathematics. The problems are short, easy to use, and fun for students.

Problem solutions involve critical thinking and careful reading of text, charts, graphs, and tables. Students are required to explain their thinking in writing.

Students are frequently asked to support their answers with evidence. The evidence cannot be uncovered by scanning the text, but instead requires in-depth analysis of the information in the text, diagram, or both. This analysis develops good reading comprehension and critical thinking skills.

The questions in *Math Detective*® are modeled after questions found on new math assessments, but require more critical thinking. These problems are excellent preparation for assessments that require students to explain and support their answers.

Also included is a chart of key ideas and topics, as well as all answers and solutions.

When to Use *Math Detective*®

Math Detective® can be used to help introduce or review topics in your math curriculum. *Math Detective*® is an ideal solution for test preparation because it does not teach to a particular assessment. It develops the skills needed to excel on new assessments. In my field-testing with students in Grades 5-6 and some older students in Grades 7-8, *Math Detective*® was highly effective in clarifying topics that they had found confusing in previous years. It is also a wonderful source of enrichment activities.

Grades 5-6 Math Standards

The math topics covered in this book are organized around the strands outlined by the National Council of Teachers of Mathematics: Number and Numeration, Operations, Geometry and Spatial Sense, Probability, Statistics and Pre-Algebra. For a detailed list of all topics covered within each of the key ideas, please see the Table of Contents (page ii) or the Key Ideas and Math Topics chart (page vi).

Many problems contain important math vocabulary. Some of these terms are defined in the problem and some must be identified through context clues in the story.

Reading in Mathematics

Many math students have trouble reading in general, and do not understand the importance of reading in mathematics. *Math Detective*® teaches students to read carefully by requiring the students to identify evidence that supports their answers. In fact, students must often identify information from multiple sources (text, diagrams, and other graphics) and synthesize these different pieces of information to arrive at the answer. The depth of analysis needed to solve these problems develops thinking skills and improves reading comprehension.

Written Explanations

Many questions in this book ask students to use complete sentences to explain their thinking. The ability to express their thoughts—supported by evidence—in writing, is not only important in math assessments, it is essential when communicating with other people in school and work. It also promotes better understanding of the mathematics being studied.

The questions in *Math Detective®* are modeled after questions found on math assessments but require more critical thinking. Despite the growing trend to evaluate written explanations and support of solutions, many math students score poorly on these test items. The carefully designed questions in *Math Detective®* will develop thinking, reading, and writing skills while they prepare your students for new state math assessments.

If a student has trouble writing about how she solved a problem, ask her to explain her solution aloud, then guide her on how to write the explanation. Remember, it helps to model your own thinking on how you solved the problem and then ask the student to model her own thinking. Showing work in a neat and organized fashion is also stressed. A separate introduction and sample problem with solutions has been provided for the student.

Thinking Cap Questions

Some problems are questions that go beyond the literal and, at times, interpretive levels of thinking. Such problems are designated by a detective cap, as shown.

KEY IDEAS and MATH TOPICS

Number & Numeration

Topic	1 Train Ride	2 Who's Who	3 Well Rounded	4 Inca Quipu	5 At the Arcade	6 The Sieve	7 Miguel's Memory	8 Walk Through Park	9 Sanchez Children
Identity		X							
Using Variables									
Odds & Evens					X	X			
Factors	X				X			X	
Multiples	X				X		X	X	
Least Common Multiples								X	
Divisibility Rules			X		X				
Primes & Composites					X	X			
Place Value			X	X					
Exponents							X		
Money Sense				X				X	
Patterns					X	X	X	X	
Addition		X	X						
Division		X							
Rounding		X							

Operations

Topic	10 Off to Movies!	11 Parking Lot	12 Potato Race	13 Camping Trails	14 Mystery Fraction	15 Rainy Week	16 Best Pancake	17 State Shopping
Decimals (+)	X	X		X				X
Decimals (−)	X			X				
Decimals (x)	X	X						X
Decimals (÷)	X							
Fractions (+)						X	X	
Fractions (−)						X		
Fractions (x)							X	
Fractions (÷)					X			
Fractions (%)								X
Addition			X					
Subtraction			X					

Geometry

Topic	18 Angle Billboards	19 Trip to Game	20 Perennial Garden	21 Quad Factory	22 Toy Box Project	23 Missing Money	24 Math Room
Types of Angles	X						
Congruency	X						
Quadrilateral Properties			X	X			
Perimeter		X	X				
Area of Rectangles		X	X			X	X
Area of Triangles						X	X
Area of Circles							X
Volume of Rectangular Prism					X		

SYNTHESIS Combines information from multiple sources to draw conclusions.

Number & Numeration: X (2) X (3) X (4) · X (6) X (7) · X (9)
Operations: X (10) X (11) X (12) X (13) X (14) X (15) X (16) X (17)
Geometry: X (19) · X (22) X (23) X (24)

OTHER MATH TOPICS

Topic (Number)	1	2	3	4	5	6	7	8	9
Multicultural			X						
History			X		X				
Decimals								X	

Topic (Operations)	10	11	12	13	14	15	16	17
Multicultural			X					
Reading a Chart	X				X			X
Graphing Fractions						X		
Measurement		X	X			X		
Time Concepts			X					
Money Sense	X	X					X	

Topic (Geometry)	18	19	20	21	22	23	24
Measurement	X	X		X			
Fractions (x,÷)				X			
Coordinate Graphing (1st Quad)						X	
Logical Reasoning	X						

KEY IDEAS and MATH TOPICS, cont.

Probability

Probability	Sum of Six 25	The Buttons 26	Spinner Game 27	Game of Dish 28	Breakfast Special 29
Finding Odds	X	X	X	X	X
Counting Principles					X

Statistics

Statistics	Great Goldfish 30	Jameel's Math 31	Cody's Graph 32	Temperature Graph 33	Making Money 34	World Record 35
Line Graph	X		X			
Double Line Graph				X		
Bar Graph		X				
Making a Bar Graph						
Circle Graphs					X	
Mean (Average)		X	X			
Interpreting Chart Data					X	

Pre-Algebra

Pre-Algebra	King Orders 36	Symbol Says 37	Missing Numbers 38	Busy Elevator 39	Function Mach. 40
Order of Operations	X				
Graphing Number Line			X		
Intro to Inequalities			X		
Addition of Integers				X	X
Concept of a Variable	X				

SYNTHESIS Combines information from multiple sources to draw conclusions.

	25	26	27	28	29		30	31	32	33	34	35		36	37	38	39	40
SYNTHESIS		X	X		X		X	X	X		X	X		X	X	X	X	

Other Math Topics

Probability

	Sum of Six 25	The Buttons 26	Spinner Game 27	Game of Dish 28	Breakfast Special 29
Concept of a Bar Graph	X				
Odds & Evens			X		
Primes & Composites			X		
Multicultural				X	
Intro to 2-stage Experiments		X			

Statistics

	Great Goldfish 30	Jameel's Math 31	Cody's Graph 32	Temperature Graph 33	Making Money 34	World Record 35
Whole Numbers (+ −)	X		X			X
Whole Numbers (+ − x ÷)		X				
Estimating				X		
Fractions (x)				X		
Measurement			X		X	
Decimals (+ -)				X		
Percent				X		
Multiples		X				

Pre-Algebra

	King Orders 36	Symbol Says 37	Missing Numbers 38	Busy Elevator 39	Function Mach. 40
Fraction Operations	X				

SCORING RUBRIC/ASSESSMENT CRITERIA

Each complete *Math Detective®* activity includes a story and questions related to that story. Questions may require arithmetic computation, identification of evidence, and explanations of the student's thinking. Therefore, to get a good picture of the student's overall performance on an activity, a 3-part scoring rubric is suggested. First, mark individual questions to indicate errors in computation, identification of evidence, and clarity of the explanations. Using a photocopy of the rubric below, combine the informal assessments to generate an overall 3-part score for the activity.

- -

Student Name _____

Activity: _____

THREE-CATEGORY SCORING RUBRIC
- Concept understanding (student understands concept, recognizes patterns)
- Clarity of student's explanations (complete sentences, clearly written)
- Correct computation of answers (accuracy of arithmetic computation)

Content: If the information in your answer showed complete understanding of the information in the story and graphics, you got a 3. If it showed a partial understanding, you got a 2 or 1. If there was absolutely no evidence that you understood the information, you got a 0.

Clarity: If you communicated clearly, even if the ideas themselves were wrong, you got a 3. If your ideas were communicated poorly, you got a 1 or 2. If you were not clear and it was impossible to understand your thoughts, you got a 0.

Accuracy: If the computation for all arithmetic problems was correct, you got a 3. If only some of it was correct, you got a 1 or 2. If none of it was correct, you got a 0.

Content Score: _____ (Scale 0–3)
Clarity Score: _____ (Scale 0–3)
Accuracy Score: _____ (Scale 0–3)

Comments:

_____

_____

_____

_____

To the Student

Why You Should Become a *Math Detective*®

Critical thinking, reading, and writing are as important in mathematics as they are in the rest of your subjects. This workbook was created to improve your thinking, reading, and writing skills while you learn and practice math!

It's All About Evidence

As a critical thinker, you need to look for *evidence* in what you read. Evidence is information that shows why something is true or could be true. Read the six sentences below and try to find the evidence that tells you who was into the peanut butter and jam.

[1]Eddie's mom looked at Eddie and baby sister Sarah. [2]There were crumbs on the floor, and Sarah had peanut butter and jam on her chin. [3]"Who got into the peanut butter and jam?" asked Eddie's mom. [4]Eddie told his mom that little Sarah had eaten the peanut butter and jam. [5]He quickly grabbed a paper towel and put some water on it so his mother could wipe Sarah's chin. [6]As he handed the towel to his mother, she noticed peanut butter and jam on Eddie's fingers.

Information in sentence 2 tell us that that "Sarah had peanut butter and jam on her chin." We know from this evidence that she was into the peanut butter and jam. Sentence 6 tells us that Eddie had peanut butter and jam on his fingers. We know from this evidence that Eddie was into the peanut butter and jam. The evidence in sentences 2 and 6 shows us that both Eddie and Sarah were into the peanut butter and jam.

The questions in these activities sometimes ask for the sentence(s) that provide the best evidence for an answer. To help you identify a particular sentence, all the sentences in the stories of this workbook are numbered. Some questions may require you to give the numbers of one or two sentences AND find information from a diagram to answer the question. You may have to go back and search the text or story for the sentence or sentences that contain the evidence you need to prove your answer is correct. All critical thinkers reread what they have read to make sure they understood what was said and to be sure they did not miss any information. In this book, YOU ARE THE DETECTIVE; that is why this book is called *Math Detective*®.

Sample Problem

The Camping Trip

[1]The Lee family was going camping. [2]Mr. and Mrs. Lee woke up at 5:30 a.m. and began to load their van with the tents, cooking utensils and suitcases. [3]Mrs. Lee began to put all the food in the cooler. [4]Mr. Lee woke up his children, Abe and Sakai, at 6:45 a.m. [5]Abe remembered to feed their dog, Bubbles. [6]Abe said: "Come on, Bubbles, eat fast! [7]Everywhere we go, you go!" [8]Sakai chose to stay in bed until the last minute. [9]The family left at 7:15 a.m. [10]As they left, Sakai said to her mom, "Mom, may I have some coffee? [11]I've been up helping for three hours." [12]Abe said, "Liar, Liar, pants on fire!" [13]Mrs. Lee said: "Now Abe, I want no fighting on this trip. [14]And as for you, young lady, you can forget about drinking coffee!"

[15]The total trip took six hours. [16]The family would have gotten there sooner but they took a 35-minute rest stop to have lunch.

Questions

1. How long were Mr. and Mrs. Lee awake before Mr. Lee woke up Abe and Sakai? _____

   Give the numbers of the two sentences that provide the best evidence for your answer. _____, _____

   Solution:

   1 hour and 15 minutes (the difference in time from 5:30 a.m. to 6:45 a.m.) Sentences 2 and 4 (Mr. and Mrs. Lee woke up at 5:30 a.m. (sentence 2); Abe and Sakai woke up at 6:45 a.m. (sentence 4).

2. What time did the family arrive at the campsite? _____

   Give the numbers of the two sentences that provide you with the best evidence for your answer. _____, _____

Solution

1:15 p.m.
Sentences 9 and 15.

(We know from sentence 9 that the family left at 7:15 a.m. and from sentence 15 that the total trip took 6 hours. Given the information in sentences 9 and 15, the solution must be 1:15 p.m. because if we add 6 hours to 7:15 a.m., we get 1:15 p.m. Therefore, sentences 9 and 15 provide the best evidence [support] for the answer.)

_____

_____

3. If the family had not stopped, at what time would they have arrived? _____
   Use complete sentences to explain your thinking.

_____

_____

Solution

12:40 p.m.

We know from question 2 that they arrived at 1:15 p.m. Sentence 16 states that the lunch break took 35 minutes. We can take 1:15 p.m. and subtract a half hour which would give us 12:45 p.m., then subtract 5 minutes from 12:45 to get the answer.

_____

_____

4. Which of the following conclusions is supported in the problem? Circle the letter of the best answer.

   a. Mr. and Mrs. Lee did all the cooking on the camping trip.

   b. Mrs. Lee does not like coffee.

   c. Bubbles, the dog, came on this trip.

   d. The family traveled by way of plane.

   Give the number of the sentence that provides the best evidence for your answer.

   _____

Solution

c.
Sentence 7
(We do know from sentence 5 that Bubbles is the dog, but in sentence 7, Abe says that everywhere the family goes, Bubbles goes. We don't know for certain that Bubbles did go, but sentence 7 provides the best evidence that Bubbles travels with the family.)

Choice a is not a good choice because we have NO evidence from the reading to know that Mr. and Mrs. Lee did all the cooking on the trip. Just because they packed a cooler doesn't mean they cooked all the food on the trip.

Choice b is not a good choice. Just because Mrs. Lee doesn't let Sakai drink coffee doesn't mean Mrs. Lee herself doesn't like coffee.

Choice d is incorrect because we have no evidence that the Lee family took a plane. We know they were loading up their van.

5. Why did Abe say: "Liar, liar, pants on fire!"? Use complete sentences to explain your thinking.

_____

_____

_____

_____

Solution

Abe said this to his sister because she was in bed until the last minute (sentence 8), so she could not have been up helping for three hours. Also, if she was awakened at 6:45 a.m. (sentence 4) and they left at 7:15 a.m. (sentence 9), then she had not been up three hours!

Math Detective® Certificate

Awarded to

_____

for _____

Signed _____

Date _____

Math Detective® Certificate

Awarded to

_____

for

_____

Signed _____

Date _____

I
NUMBER & NUMERATION

1—The Train Ride

[1]Mrs. Applecrumb, Mrs. Winterbloom, Mr. Papas, Ms. Kamen, Ms. Twinkle, and Mr. Lyons were in the same train car. [2]Mrs. Applecrumb sat in seat 10. [3]Mrs. Winterbloom sat in seat 5 next to Mr. Papas, who sat in seat 6. [4]Ms. Kamen always sat in the back on the last seat, seat 27, because she liked to stretch her legs and grade her students' papers. [5]Ms. Twinkle sat in seat 20 next to Mr. Lyons, who sat in seat 19.

[6]The train engineer loved to play math games during the ride. [7]He said over the loud speaker, "Does anyone know what a factor is?" [8]Mrs. Winterbloom, who was not really listening, said, "This man is silly. [9]Of course, I know what a tractor is." [10]Mr. Papas laughed and explained to her that the word was "factor" not "tractor." [11]The train engineer then said, "If any of you are seated in a seat that is a factor of 20, you will get a free engineer's cap. [12]Now remember, my fellow riders, a factor is any number that goes into another number evenly or without a remainder." [13]He explained, "Remember, the factors of 12 are 1, 2, 3, 4, 6 and 12. [14]Don't get this confused with the word m-u-l-t-i-p-l-e (he said this word very slowly). [15]The multiples of 12 are 12, 24, 36, 48, 60, etc., etc." [16]Mr. Lyons became very happy. [17]He began to shout, "I am seated on a seat that is a factor of 20." [18]This made Ms. Kamen very upset. [19]She began to mumble to herself and shake her head.

[20]Then the engineer said, "By the way, any of you who are seated in a seat that is a multiple of 1 will get a free ride next time."

Questions

1. What are the factors of 20? _____

   Give the number of the sentence that provides the best evidence for your answer. _____

2. Of the people mentioned in the story, who will get a free engineer's cap on this ride? Use complete sentences to explain your thinking.

   _____

   _____

   _____

3. Is Mr. Lyons correct in thinking that he will be getting a free engineer's cap on this ride? Why or why not? Use complete sentences to explain your thinking.

_____

_____

_____

4. Which of the following shows the first four multiples of 3?

    a. 3, 6, 9, and 12

    b. 3, 9, 12, and 18

    c. 1, 3, 6, and 9

    d. none of these

    Give the number of the sentence that provides the best evidence for your answer.

    _____

5. Of the people mentioned in the story, who is seated in a seat that is a multiple of 3?

    _____

6. Why is 1 a factor of every number? Use complete sentences to explain your thinking.

    _____

    _____

    _____

    _____

7. Who will be getting a free ride next time they ride the train?

    a. Ms. Kamen

    b. Mr. Papas and Ms. Twinkle

    c. Mrs. Applecrumb

    d. all of them

2—Who's Who?

[1]Each figure stands for a whole number in all four equations. [2]A whole number is a number that is not a fraction or a decimal. [3]These are the whole numbers: {0, 1, 2, 3, ...}.

[4]In the chart below, the same figure always stands for the same number. [5]Can you find who's who? [6]Answer the questions below as you do.

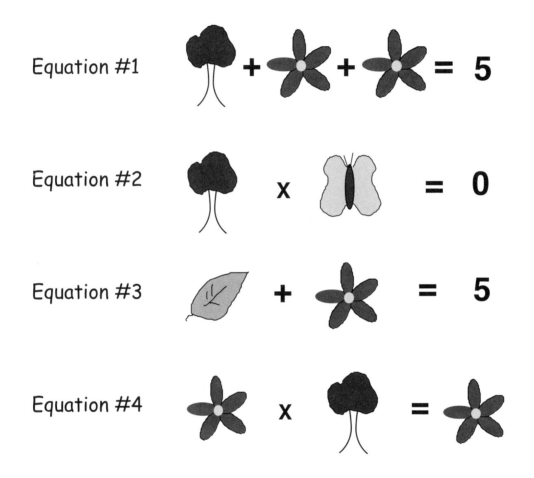

Equation #1

Equation #2

Equation #3

Equation #4

Questions

As you find the value of an object, write it above each of its drawings.

1. In Equation #4, since the flower times the tree equals the flower, what whole number is represented by the tree? _____ Use a complete sentence to explain your thinking.

_____

_____

_____

2. In Equation #1, each flower represents the same whole number. What whole number is represented by the flower? _____ Use complete sentences to explain your thinking.

_____

_____

_____

3. In Equation #2, what whole number is represented by the butterfly? _____ Use complete sentences to explain your thinking.

_____

_____

_____

4. In Equation # 3, what whole number is represented by the leaf? (Circle the correct answer.)

   a. 2

   b. 0

   c. 3

   d. 1

5. The whole number 0 is called the *identity* for addition. Which of the following explains why 0 is called the identity for addition?

   When you:

   a. Add 0 to any number, you get 0.

   b. Add 0 to any number, you get the number you started with.

   c. Multiply any number by 0, you get 1.

   d. Divide any number by 0, you get the number you started with.

6. The whole number 1 is called the *identity* for multiplication. Why do you think that is? Use complete sentences to explain your thinking.

_____

_____

3—Well Rounded

[1]Daycia, Luis, Joey, and Mary each got a four-digit number to round to the nearest thousand. [2]Mary said, "When my number is rounded to the nearest thousand it is 5,000." [3]Luis said, "That's funny, when my number is rounded to the nearest thousand it is also 5,000, but my number before rounding is different from your number." [4]Mary said to Luis, "My number is divisible by 3, which means it can be divided by 3 with no remainders, and yours is not divisible by 3!" [5]Luis said, "How do you know that without dividing it?" [6]Mary said, "When I add the digits of my number, I get a number that 3 goes into evenly, so that means my number is divisible by 3!" [7]Daycia said, "She's right because my number happens to be a third of Mary's number." [8]Joey said, "My number is the sum of Mary's and Luis's numbers."

Remember—a sum is the answer to an addition problem.

Name	thousands	hundreds	tens	ones
	4	7	3	1
	4	9	1	5
Joey				
Daycia				

Questions

1. Which four-digit number shown on the table above is Mary's number? Use complete sentences to explain your thinking.

   _____

   _____

   _____

Give the numbers of the two sentences that provide the best evidence for your answer. _____, _____

2. a. Which is Luis's number? _____

   b. Prove that Luis's number is NOT divisible by 3. Show your work.

3. Find Daycia's number. Write it on the chart. Show your work.

   Give the number of the sentence that provides the best evidence for your answer. _____

4. Find Joey's number. Write it on the chart. Show your work.

   Give the number of the sentence that provides the best evidence for your answer. _____

5. Show that Joey's number and Daycia's number are not divisible by 3.

6. Are any of the numbers divisible by 2 or 5? _____ Use complete sentences to explain your thinking.

   _____

   _____

7. Round Joey's number and Daycia's number to the nearest thousand.

   Joey's number rounded to the nearest thousand is _____.

   Daycia's number rounded to the nearest thousand is _____.

4—The Inca Quipu

[1]The Inca civilization ruled in parts of South America from 1400 to 1560. [2]The Incas had no written language as far as we know. [3]They kept all their records by using long cotton or wool strings tied with many different knots. [4]These strings or cords are called quipus.

[5]A quipu had one main cord with many cords hanging from it. [6]The Incas used many different colors for their cords. [7]The quipus were mostly used to keep records of crops and population. [8]Some quipus had as many as 2,000 cords! [9]The quipus were folded and carried from city to city. [10]In this way, data or information was able to be communicated from place to place. [11]Because of this, quipu makers were very important to their society.

[12]The Incas used a decimal (base 10) number system just as we do. [13]In base 10, the number 6354 means (6 x 1,000) + (3 x 100) + (5 x 10) + (4 x 1). [14]This way of writing a number by showing the place value of each digit is called **expanded notation**. [15]In a quipu, each knot represents a digit. [16]Where the knots are placed represents its place value. [17]The quipu was not used as a calculator but as an instrument to store information. [18]The Incas knew the importance of numbers and had a very advanced system of record keeping. [19]Study this quipu diagram below.

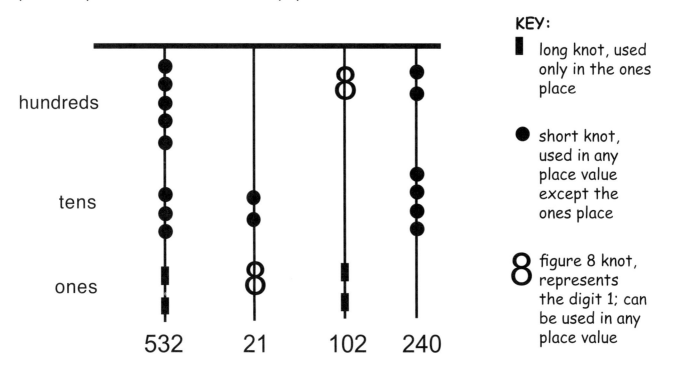

hundreds

tens

ones

532   21   102   240

KEY:

▮ long knot, used only in the ones place

● short knot, used in any place value except the ones place

8 figure 8 knot, represents the digit 1; can be used in any place value

Source: Ascher, Robert and Marcia, <u>Code of the Quipu</u>. Ann Arbor: The University of Michigan Press, 1981.

Questions

1. How many years did the Incas rule?_____ Show your work.

   Give the number of the sentence that provides the best evidence for your answer.
   _____

2. Was the quipu used to multiply and divide numbers? _____ Why or why not?
   Explain with one complete sentence.

   _____

   Give the number of the sentence that provides the best evidence for your answer.
   _____

3. Based on the text, which is true? Circle the letter of the best answer.

   a. The Incas used ink and paper to keep crop and population records.

   b. The Incas used a number system with the same base that we use.

   c. The Incas left many books explaining their civilization.

   d. You would need 11 knots to represent the number 11.

   Give the number of the sentence that provides the best evidence for your answer.
   _____

4. Write this number in expanded notation: 4,231

   _____

5. What number is (8 x 1,000) + (3 x 10) + (5 x 1)? _____

6. What is the smallest number a quipu with eight knots using two place values can
   represent?_____

   Use complete sentences to explain your thinking.

   _____

   _____

7. In Inca City A there are 513 people. In Inca City B there are 605 people, and in Inca City C there are only 21 people. Finish drawing the quipu below to record this information. Use the diagram on page 8 to help you. You may use colors.

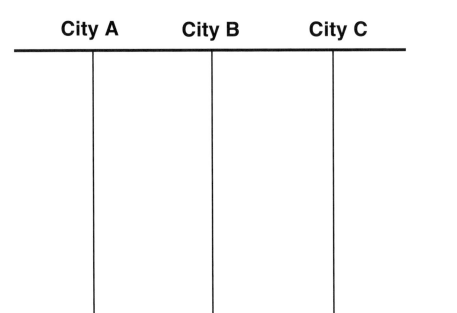

City A   **City B**   **City C**

5—At The Arcade

[1]Mark and Luis were at the game arcade at the mall. [2]The machines at the arcade accept only nickels—and each game costs only one nickel. [3]Mark said to Luis, "I have 16 cents in my pocket and only 8 coins." [4]Luis said, "I have 8 cents in my pocket and also only 8 coins. [5]So if you have twice as much money as I do, you must have twice as many coins as I do." [6]Then Mark said, "Let's empty out our pockets and count to see if we have enough to play three more games. [7]Maybe we need to go get change."

Questions

1. How many coins do the boys need if they want to play three more games? _____

   Give the number of the sentence that helps you find the cost of playing three games. _____ How much will playing three games cost? _____

2. List the possible coins that Mark could have if he has 16 cents. In your list, circle the combination that has 8 coins.

3. List the possible coins that Luis could have if he has 8 cents. Circle the combination that has 8 coins.

4. What kinds of coins do Mark and Luis have? Write one complete sentence.

   _____

   _____

5. Is Luis correct in thinking Mark has twice as many coins? _____ Why or why not?

   _____

   _____

   _____

6. If the boys put their coins together, without going to get change, how many more games can they play? _____ Explain your thinking with complete sentences.

_____

_____

_____

Story, continued:

[8]Mark decided to find his sister Maria, who was outside having pizza with her friends. [9]He asked her if she had any coins in her purse. [10]Maria said, " I have twelve coins left, which make a total of 25 cents." [11]Maria also said to her brother, "Mark, the change machine is broken, but I might be able to give you at least one nickel."

7. List all the possible coins that add up to 25 cents. Circle the combination on your list that has 12 coins.

8. Give the number of the sentence that helps you find which coins Maria had. _____ What kinds of coins did she have?

_____

9. How many nickels was Maria able to give her brother? _____ Explain your thinking.

_____

_____

6—The Sieve of Eratosthenes

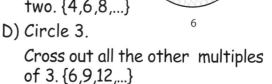

[1]Eratosthenes, a famous mathematician, developed a way of finding prime numbers by a method now called the Sieve* of Eratosthenes. [2]A prime number is any whole number after the number 1 that has only two factors, one and itself. [3]Eratosthenes was born in Cyrene, North Africa (now known as Lybia), in 276 B.C. [4]He died in Egypt in 194 B.C.

[5]This is how you start the sieve:

A) Start by crossing out 1. One is not a prime number.

B) Circle 2. Two is the first prime number.

C) Cross out all the other multiples of two. {4,6,8,...}

D) Circle 3.

Cross out all the other multiples of 3. {6,9,12,...}

E) Circle 5 (since 4 was crossed out). Cross out all the other multiples of 5.

F) Circle 7 (since 6 was crossed out). Cross out all the other multiples of 7.

[6]Continue doing this until you cross out all the composite numbers and all that you have left in the sieve are the circled prime numbers!

*A sieve is used to sift, or separate.

1	2	3	4	5	6	7	8	9	10
11	12	13	14	15	16	17	18	19	20
21	22	23	24	25	26	27	28	29	30
31	32	33	34	35	36	37	38	39	40
41	42	43	44	45	46	47	48	49	50
51	52	53	54	55	56	57	58	59	60
61	62	63	64	65	66	67	68	69	70
71	72	73	74	75	76	77	78	79	80
81	82	83	84	85	86	87	88	89	90
91	92	93	94	95	96	97	98	99	100

Questions

1. How old was Eratosthenes when he died? _____ Show your work.

   Give the numbers of the sentences that provide the best evidence for your answer. _____, _____

2. What is a composite number? Use your own words.

   _____

   _____

3. Which of these statements is NOT true?

   a. Two is the only even prime.

   b. Composite numbers are not prime.

   c. Prime numbers go on forever.

   d. One is a prime number.

4. What do the multiples of 5 have in common? Explain with complete sentences.

   _____

   _____

5. What is an easy way to tell which numbers are multiples of 11? Look at the sieve and explain.

   _____

   _____

6. Why is the number 200 not a prime number? Use complete sentences to explain your thinking.

   _____

   _____

   _____

7—Miguel's Memory Games

[1]Lucy, Maria, Gary, and Emily were the only friends at Miguel's birthday party. [2]While some of them were watching a video on TV, Miguel turned to one of them. [3]"We've seen this movie before, so let's play a memory game," Miguel said. [4]He added, "You start with the first letter of your name and then say every other letter of the alphabet after that. [5]I will start with my age and say <u>every</u> <u>other</u> odd number after that. [6]We'll take turns and whoever gets the wrong answer first, loses the game!"

This is how they started:

E, 11, G, 15, _____, _____, _____, _____, _____, _____, _____, _____

Questions

1. What is Miguel's age? _____ Give the number of the sentence that best supports your answer. _____

2. Who is Miguel playing this game with? _____ Give the number of the sentence that provides the best evidence for your answer. _____

3. a. Finish the pattern above.

   b. At one point Miguel said "29" and his friend said the letter "O." Who lost the game? _____. Explain why with a complete sentence.

   _____

   _____

Story, continued:

[7]Then when the movie was over, Miguel and Gary decided to play a different game. [8]Miguel said, "You start with the first prime number and I'll say the next prime number. [9]We'll take turns doing this. [10]Whoever misses a prime number or says a composite number will lose."

[11]Gary started correctly with 2, and Miguel said 3. [12]Gary said 5 and Miguel said 7 and both continued saying the prime numbers correctly until Gary said 47 and Miguel said 51. [13]Emily and Lucy, who were listening, stopped the game and said, "One of you said a composite number!" [14]After a little while, the game stopped and they all went to the kitchen to eat cake and ice cream.

4. What is the first prime number? _____ Give the number of the sentence or
    sentences that provide the best evidence for your answer. _____

5. What is a prime number? Use complete sentences to explain your thinking.

    _____

    _____

6. From your reading of sentence 10, what do you think a composite number is? Use
    complete sentences to explain your thinking.

    _____

    _____

    _____

    _____

7. a. Make a list of the prime numbers less than 60.

    b. Who lost the second game? Why? Use complete sentences to explain your
    thinking.

    _____

    _____

    _____

8.   How could you prove to someone that 57 and 111 are prime numbers or not
    prime numbers?

    _____

    _____

    _____

8—A Walk Through the Park

[1]Sofia and Pepin walked with their grandfather through the park after school. [2]The grandfather pointed to some branches on an old tree. [3]He said, "Imagine that each of those two branches will someday make two more branches. [4]Then, those brand new branches will each make two new branches and so on and so on." [5]Sofia said, "Yes, it's like people having children and those children having more children..." [6]Grandfather said, "Yes, those larger branches were once little branches. [7]I'm sure my own grandfather looked at them when he was small." [8]Pepin said, " So, for example 2 + 2 + 2 + 2 = 8. [9]Maybe by the time I'm older there might be 8 new branches." [10]"No, it's more branches than that. [11]I'll draw you a picture when I get home," the grandfather said.

[12]When the children got home, the grandfather drew a picture of 2 x 2 x 2 x 2. [13]Then he said, "This is also written as 2^4 where the 2 is called the base, just like the base or trunk of a tree. [14]It is read as two to the fourth power. [15]The little 4 is called the exponent. [16]The exponent tells you how many times to multiply the base times itself. [17]Trees don't always make two branches each time, but this should give you a good idea of why some trees, and also some families, get so big!"

Questions

1. Give the numbers of the two sentences that provide the best evidence of how the branches multiply. _____, _____ Continue the drawing to show 2^4. (The two branches show 2^1.)

2. Using the drawing you made, fill out this list to show how many branches are in each generation. (The first is done for you!)

		Number of Branches
First generation	2 x 1	2
Second generation	2 x 2	____
Third generation	2 x 2 x 2	____
Fourth generation	2 x 2 x 2 x 2	____

3. How many branches are there in total after four generations? _____
Show your work.

4. Do you agree with the grandfather that Pepin is incorrect in his thinking? Why or why not? Explain in complete sentences.

_____

_____

5. Give the number of the sentence that tells you what the 3 is called in the number 3^5. _____What is it called? _____

6. Give the number of the sentence that tells you what the 5 is called in the number 3^5. _____What is it called? _____

7. What does the exponent tell you to do to the base? _____

_____

Give the number of the sentence that provides the best evidence for your answer. _____

8. How would you read 2^5? _____

Give the number of the sentence that provides the best evidence for your answer. _____

9. Do the branches of a tree always grow in groups of two? _____ Give the number of the sentence that provides the best evidence for your answer. _____

Story, continued:

[18]Later in the day, the grandfather made these cards to play a game with Sofia and Pepin. [19]He asked them to put these cards in order from smallest to largest.

10. Put these cards in order from smallest to largest, using the cutouts on the next page. Show your work.

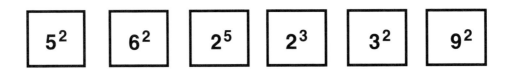

5^2 6^2 2^5 2^3 3^2 9^2

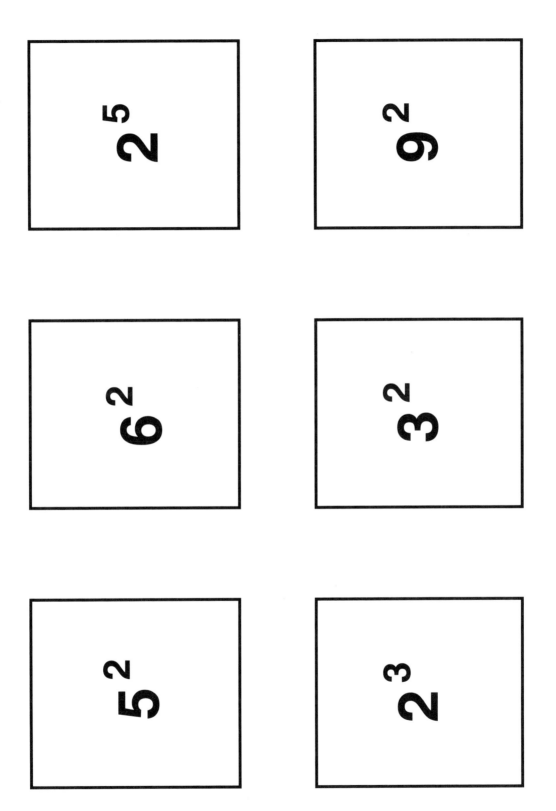

2^5

9^2

6^2

3^2

5^2

2^3

9—Mrs. Sanchez's Four Children

[1]Mrs. Sanchez's four children wanted to earn an allowance during the summer. [2]Mrs. Sanchez decided that she would pay them an allowance if they did chores for thirty days. [3]This way the children would have spending money for their vacation in August. [4]Mrs. Sanchez decided to post a list of chores on a clipboard.

[5]On the first day of the summer, the family had a meeting and the children chose their jobs. [6]Juan chose to bathe the dogs. [7]Luis chose to do the laundry. [8]The older sister, Veronica, decided to wash the windows. [9]Maria, who loves to vacuum, chose vacuuming.

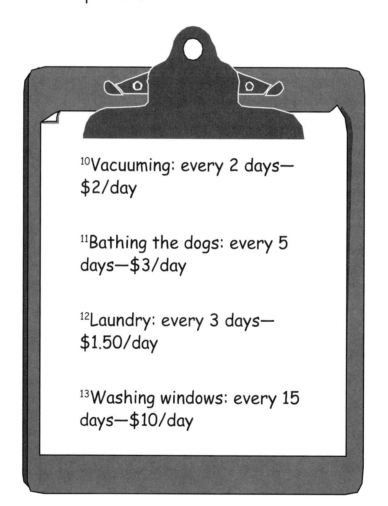

[10]Vacuuming: every 2 days—$2/day

[11]Bathing the dogs: every 5 days—$3/day

[12]Laundry: every 3 days—$1.50/day

[13]Washing windows: every 15 days—$10/day

Questions

1. Based on the information in the clipboard, fill out the chart on the next page. Use it to answer the questions that follow.

Mrs. Sanchez's Four Children

Fill out this chart based on your reading.

Name	How often: every…	1	2	3	4	5	6	7	8	9	10	11	12	13	14	15	16	17	18	19	20	21	22	23	24	25	26	27	28	29	30
	vacuum ___ 2 days		X																													
	___ 3 days			X																												
	___ 5 days					X																										
	___ 15 days															X																

The first "x" represents the day Mrs. Sanchez's children started their chores. Continue marking an "x" on the day that each child does his or her chore.

2. How much money will Luis make in thirty days? _____. Show your work.

Which two sentences best support your answer? _____, _____

3. How often will Maria and Luis be working on the same day? _____

4. How often will Maria and Juan be working on the same day? _____

5. How often will all children be working on the same day? _____

6. Find the least common multiple of 2, 3, 5, and 15. (The Least Common Multiple, or LCM, is the smallest multiple that all of these numbers have in common.) Start listing the multiples of these numbers until you find the least common multiple of the four numbers. Circle the LCM.

   Multiples of 2_____

   Multiples of 3_____

   Multiples of 5_____

   Multiples of 15 _____

7. If all the children did all their chores, find who made the most money at the end of the month. _____ Show your work neatly. Write in complete sentences to explain your answer.

   _____

   _____

II
OPERATIONS

10—Off to the Movies!

[1]Lucy, Melissa, and Amy decided to go to the matinee movies on Sunday. [2]The regular movie price is $7.00 per person, but $5.00 is the price for the Sunday matinee.

[3]Lucy brought $16.00. [4]Melissa brought $14.00. [5]Amy had $6.50. [6]They decided to put all their money together to pay for the movie and buy all they wanted to eat. [7]Each girl got a different size soda. [8]They decided to buy only one candy bar and share it among the three of them. [9]They each bought their own popcorn. [10]Amy bought the medium popcorn. [11]After paying for the movies and all the food they realized that they had spent all their money!

Trapezoid Theatre Snack Menu

Extra Large Popcorn	$6.00	Candy bar	$2.00
Medium Popcorn	4.50	Coffee	1.25
Small Popcorn	4.00	Hot Tea	1.00
Large Soda	3.50		
Medium Soda	2.00	**Our Popcorn is**	
Small Soda	1.50	**Always Fresh!**	

Questions

1. How much money did the girls spend on the movie tickets? _____ Show your work.

   Give the numbers of the two sentences that provide the best evidence for your answer. _____, _____

2. Before spending any money, how much did the girls have altogether? _____ Show your work.

3. How much did the three girls spend on soda? _____ Show your work.

Give the number of the sentence that provides the best evidence for your answer. _____

4. How much did the girls spend in total for the movie, sodas, and candy bar? _____ Show your work.

5. How much money do they have left over for popcorn? _____ Show your work.

6. What size popcorn did Melissa and Lucy buy? _____ Use complete sentences to explain your thinking.

_____

_____

_____

_____

7. If at the end, one of the girls had found three dollars in her purse, would they have had enough money to buy Lucy and Melissa each an extra large popcorn? _____ Use complete sentences to explain your thinking.

_____

_____

_____

_____

11—The Parking Lot Problem

[1]Alexis and Veni drove to Philadelphia for the weekend. [2]They decided to see some of the sights, and they needed a place to park for $3\frac{1}{2}$ hours. [3]These are the signs they saw at two different parking lots:

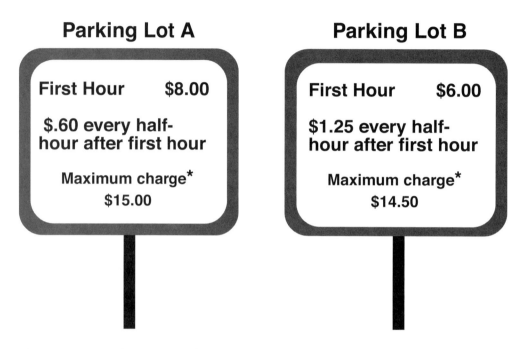

Parking Lot A

First Hour $8.00

$.60 every half-hour after first hour

Maximum charge*
$15.00

Parking Lot B

First Hour $6.00

$1.25 every half-hour after first hour

Maximum charge*
$14.50

*Maximum charge is the most you can be charged in one day, no matter how long you park.

Questions

1. Finish the chart below.

	Parking Lot A	**Parking Lot B**
First Hour	$8.00	
Second Hour	+ $1.20	+
Third Hour	+	+
Half-hour	+	+
Total		

2. Which parking lot offers the better deal for the time Alexis and Veni need to park?_____ Use complete sentences to explain why.

_____

_____

3. If Alexis and Veni needed to park for 7 hours, which lot would be the better deal? _____ How much would they pay in total? _____ Use complete sentences to explain your thinking.

_____

_____

4. Why do you think parking lots charge more for the first hour? Use complete sentences to explain.

_____

_____

12—The Potato Race

[1]Mrs. Sanchez told her students that today they were going to play a game she used to play when she was a child growing up in Cuba. [2]She said, "This game is called the Potato Game." [3]She explained, "Each of you will try to pick up 5 potatoes, one at a time, with one big spoon. [4]Then take each one on the spoon over to a bucket 20 feet away. [5]When you drop one in the bucket, you come back and get the next one. [6]But, you must have one arm behind your back at all times. [7]You may not use any part of your body or any object, other than the spoon itself, to help get the potato onto the spoon. [8]The person with the best time bringing all five potatoes into the bucket is the winner." [9]She then said, "Running is not a good idea because you may drop your potato!"

[10]Mrs. Sanchez picked Emily, Eddy, Amanda, and Luis to begin the race. [11]Eddy finished the race in 8 minutes. [12]He tried to run and dropped each of his potatoes. [13]It took him a long time to get each one back on his spoon! [14]Amanda was 35 seconds faster than Emily. [15]Luis bragged that this game was too easy, but he finished 50 seconds after Amanda. [16]Help Mrs. Sanchez finish the chart she started.

Emily	4 min 15 sec
Eddy	
Amanda	
Luis	

Questions

1. Find how long it took Amanda to finish the race. Show your work.

Give the number of the sentence that provides the best evidence for your answer.

_____

2. Find how long it took Luis to finish the race. Show your work.

Give the number of the sentence that provides the best evidence for your answer. _____

3. Who won the Potato Race out of the first four students who tried it?

   a. Amanda
   b. Eddy
   c. Emily
   d. Luis

4. Ramón, the fastest student in Mrs. Sanchez's class, finished the Potato Race in only 1 minute and 20 seconds! How much less time is that when compared to Eddy, who came in last? _____ Show your work.

5. Vicky, another student in Mrs. Sanchez's class, pushed the potato onto the spoon by using her foot. Why did Mrs. Sanchez not allow her to finish the race? Use complete sentences to explain your thinking.

   _____

   _____

   _____

   Give the number of the sentence that provides the best evidence for your answer. _____

13—The Camping Trails

[1]Frank and his family went on a camping trip with Eddy and his family. [2]The campground they stayed in is famous for its beautiful waterfall. [3]Also, there are many trails for horseback riding, a large swimming pool, and a nice clean lake called Lake Agua Clara. [4]Lake Agua Clara is 1.6 miles from the entrance along Trail 1. [5]Frank and his family stayed in Campground A, and Eddy and his family stayed in Campground B. [6]Road 1, which goes from the entrance to Campground A, is 2.8 miles. [7]Road 2, which goes from the entrance to Campground B, is 2 miles. [8]From Campground B to Campground A along Trail 3 is 1.4 miles.

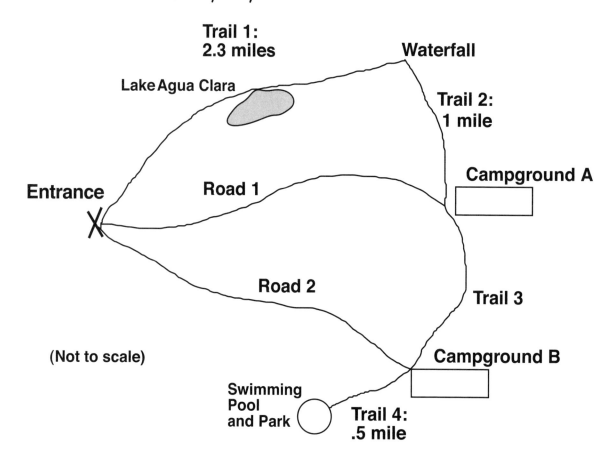

Trail 1: 2.3 miles

Waterfall

Lake Agua Clara

Trail 2: 1 mile

Campground A

Entrance

Road 1

Road 2

Trail 3

Campground B

(Not to scale)

Swimming Pool and Park

Trail 4: .5 mile

Questions

1. Eddy hiked from Campground B to Campground A to pick up Frank, and together they walked to the waterfall. How many miles did Eddy hike? _____ Show your work.

2. How far would Eddy and Frank have to hike to go from the waterfall to Lake Agua Clara? _____ Show your work.

3. A mile is 5,280 feet. How many feet is Road 2? _____ Show your work.

    Give the number of the sentence that provides the best evidence for your answer. _____

4. How far is the swimming pool from the waterfall by way of Trails 2, 3, and 4? _____ Show your work.

5. ⚑ From Lake Agua Clara, Eddy and Frank were wondering which way would be a shorter hike back to Campground B. Would it be closer to go by the entrance and then down Road 2, or would it be shorter to go back to the waterfall and down Trails 2 and 3? _____ Show your work. Use complete sentences to explain your thinking.

    _____

    _____

    _____

14—The Mystery Fraction

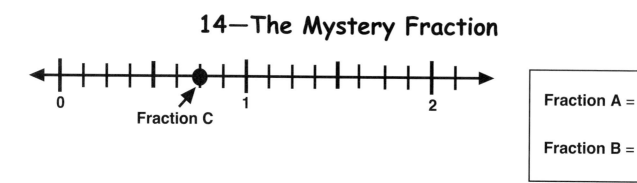

Fraction C

Fraction A = $\frac{7}{8}$

Fraction B = $\frac{3}{4}$

Questions

1. Why is fraction A less than 1?

   a. Because $\frac{7}{8}$ is to the right of 1.

   b. Because all fractions are smaller than 1.

   c. Because $\frac{7}{8}$ is less than $\frac{8}{8}$, which is 1.

   d. None of these.

2. Which fraction is bigger, Fraction A or Fraction B? _____ Using a complete sentence, support your answer by giving a good reason.

   _____

   _____

3. Which fraction is bigger, Fraction B or Fraction C? _____ Using a complete sentence, support your answer by giving a good reason.

   _____

   _____

4. Fraction D is the sum of Fraction A + Fraction B. What is Fraction D? _____ Show your work.

5. Graph and label fractions A, B, and D on the number line above (if you haven't already done so).

6. Fraction X is a mystery fraction. It is less than Fraction D but greater than 1. Name a fraction that could be Fraction X, using the number line on page 32 to help you. Explain in a complete sentence why you chose Fraction X.

_____

_____

7. Find a fraction that is between Fraction D and Fraction X. Explain how you found it.

_____

_____

_____

15—The Rainy Week

[1]It had not rained at all during the spring. [2]Now that school was out, it just kept raining and raining! [3]One weather station reported that it would rain every day for the next seven days. [4]It also said that cities closer to the ocean would get more rain than cities that were farther away from the ocean. [5]Many people were afraid of flooding. [6]People who lived in City A were told that flooding would not happen unless it rained more than 6 inches. [7]People in City B were told that flooding would happen if and only if it rained more than 8 inches.

[8]A week later the same weather station reported the rainfalls (in inches) of these two nearby cities.

	City A	City B
Monday 7/1	2	4
Tuesday 7/2	1	$1\frac{1}{4}$
Wednesday 7/3	0	$1\frac{1}{2}$
Thursday 7/4	$\frac{1}{4}$	0
Friday 7/5	0	$1\frac{3}{4}$
Saturday 7/6	$\frac{1}{4}$	1
Sunday 7/7	$\frac{1}{8}$	$\frac{1}{4}$

From: *The Manatee Journal* July 8, 2002

Questions

1. Give the total rainfall amounts for both City A and City B for the week. Show your work.

   City A   **City B**

2. What data on the chart does not agree with the weather station's prediction? Use complete sentences to explain your thinking.

   _____

   _____

3. Which type of measurement was the weather station using? _____

    a. feet
    b. inches
    c. centimeters
    d. yards

    Give the number of the sentence that provides the best evidence for your answer.
    _____

4. On which day did it rain the same amount in both cities? _____

5. How much more did it rain in City B than City A on July 6th? _____
    Show your work.

6. If the weather station was correct, did City A suffer any flooding? _____ Give
    the number of the sentence that best supports your answer. _____ Use complete
    sentences to explain your thinking.

    _____

    _____

7. a. If the weather station was correct, did City B suffer any flooding? _____ Give
    the number of the sentence that best supports your answer. _____ Use complete
    sentences to explain your thinking.

    _____

    _____

    b. What is the difference between flood level and what City B got? _____ Show
    your work.

8. If the weather station was correct, which city do you expect was closer to
    the ocean? _____ Give the number of the sentence that best supports
    your answer. _____

9. Suppose that on July 8th, the total amount of rainfall for both cities was
    2 inches. If City A got $\frac{1}{4}$ of an inch, how much did City B get? _____ Show your
    work.

16—The Best Pancake Recipe

[1]Olga is having eleven friends over for a slumber party. [2]She wants to make her mom's best pancake recipe. [3]This is the recipe:

1 c flour

1 c buttermilk

1 $\frac{1}{3}$ T sugar

1 t baking powder

$\frac{1}{2}$ t baking soda

$\frac{1}{2}$ t salt

1 T vegetable oil

1 egg

[4]Combine the flour, baking powder, baking soda, salt, and sugar in a medium bowl. [5]Then, add the buttermilk, egg, and oil. [6]Mix by hand until blended. [7]The batter will be lumpy. [8]Heat a little oil in a skillet on medium heat. [9]When the oil is hot, pour the mixture and flatten each pancake a little with a spoon. [10]Turn only when the edges look done and bubbles begin to form on the top, which allows it to hold together. [11]Enjoy with pure maple syrup! [12]Makes nine 4-inch pancakes (serves 3–4 people).

[13]Olga's mom reminds her that 1 tablespoon (T) is the same as 3 teaspoons (t). [14]She also reminds Olga that four cups of liquid is the same as one quart.

Questions

1. Give the number of the sentence that tells you how many friends are coming to the slumber party. _____ How many friends are coming? _____

2. If each person eats 3 pancakes, how many people can eat from this recipe? _____ Give the number of the sentence that provides the best evidence for your answer. _____

3. If each person including Olga eats 3 pancakes, how many pancakes should Olga make? _____

4. By how much should Olga multiply this recipe to have enough pancakes? Use a complete sentence.

_____

_____

5. Change the recipe to make three pancakes for each of the twelve children.

_____ flour   _____ baking soda

_____ buttermilk   _____ salt

_____ sugar   _____ vegetable oil

_____ baking powder   _____ eggs

6. What fraction of a dozen eggs will Olga need for the new recipe? _____

7. How many quarts of buttermilk will she need for the new recipe? _____ Give the number of the sentence that provides the best evidence for your answer. _____

8. How many tablespoons of baking powder will be needed for the new recipe? _____ Give the number of the sentence that provides the best evidence for your answer. _____

9. Olga mixed the flour with the buttermilk and then added the other ingredients. Did Olga follow the instructions in the recipe? _____ Use complete sentences to explain your thinking.

_____

_____

Give the numbers of the two sentences that provide the best evidence for your answer. _____, _____

10. When Olga turned her first pancake, the pancake fell apart! What do you think she might have done wrong? Use complete sentences to explain your thinking.

_____

_____

_____

Give the number of the sentence that provides the best evidence for your answer. _____

17—The 2002 State Shopping Spree

[1]"Imagine you could spend a week shopping, going from state to state looking for the best bargains," said Trish. [2]She added, "Some states require you to pay more in sales tax than others do. [3]Tammy said, "We would have to find out the sales tax rate in each state in order to find the best bargain." [4]Trish then said, "Let's pretend we can travel from state to state. [5]We can look up the sales tax rates on the Internet."

[6]To the right are the states that Trish and Tammy looked up. [7]Trish said, "I think I'll move to Alaska. [8]Everything will be cheaper in a state that has no tax." [9]Tammy said, "I'm not sure that is always true. "

FACT	State	Tax Rate
#1	Alaska	0 %
#2	California	8 %
#3	Delaware	0 %
#4	Florida	7 %
#5	Montana	0 %
#6	New Hampshire	0 %
#7	New York	8 %
#8	North Carolina	6 %
#9	North Dakota	5 %
#10	Oregon	0 %
#11	South Carolina	6 %
#12	South Dakota	5 %
#13	Virginia	4 %

Questions

To answer the questions, assume there are no other fees or taxes.

1. The same bicycle costs $250 in California and in New York. In which of these two states will you have to pay more sales tax? _____ Use one complete sentence to explain your thinking.

   _____

   _____

   Which two facts provide the best evidence for your answer?_____, _____

2. What tax would you pay in New York or in California for this bike? _____ Show your work. Don't forget that to change 8% to a decimal, you write .08 (because .08 is 8 hundredths).

3. The same notebook costs $5.99 in both New York and Virginia. By how much will the tax differ?_____

   a. The tax will be the same in both states.
   b. The tax in New York will be half as much as in Virginia.
   c. The tax will be twice as much in New York as in Virginia.
   d. None of the above.

   Which two facts on the chart provide the best evidence for your answer? _____, _____

4. In Oregon, a TV costs $299.25. In North Dakota, the same TV costs $285.00. Including tax, how much would you pay in each state? _____ Show your work.

   In which state should you buy the TV? Use complete sentences to explain your thinking. _____

   _____

5. Compare how much a person would pay in taxes for the same $20,000 car in these three states: Virginia, Florida and Delaware. Show your work.

   Virginia   Florida   Delaware

6. On the chart below, list the total costs of the $20,000 car, including the sales tax, by state (Virginia, Florida, Delaware). List costs in order, beginning with the least expensive. Show your work.

State	Cost

7. Do you agree with Trish that "Everything will be cheaper in a state that has no sales tax"? Use complete sentences to explain your thinking.

_____

_____

8. Trish wanted to buy these items in North Carolina: A beach umbrella ($5.00), suntan lotion ($9.00), and a beach towel ($12.00).

In which case would Trish pay more:
1) She finds the tax for each item first and then adds the total?
2) She adds the cost of all the items and then finds the sales tax on that total?

Show your work. Use complete sentences to explain your thinking.

_____

_____

_____

_____

III
GEOMETRY

18—Angle Billboards

HELP US FIND THE MISSING ANGLES! Carefully study these billboards. Do not measure!

Billboard 1

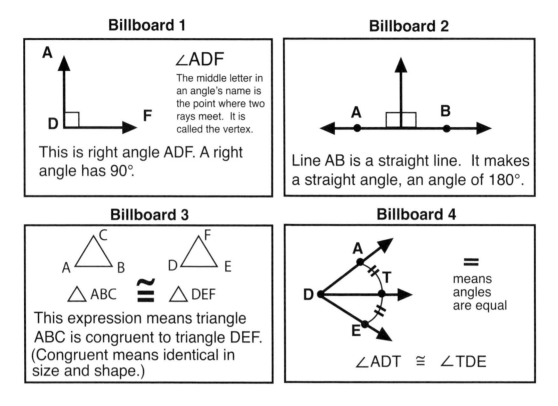

∠ADF

The middle letter in an angle's name is the point where two rays meet. It is called the vertex.

This is right angle ADF. A right angle has 90°.

Billboard 2

Line AB is a straight line. It makes a straight angle, an angle of 180°.

Billboard 3

△ ABC ≅ △ DEF

This expression means triangle ABC is congruent to triangle DEF. (Congruent means identical in size and shape.)

Billboard 4

= means angles are equal

∠ADT ≅ ∠TDE

Questions

1. Find the measure of ∠ CBE. _____ Use complete sentences to explain your thinking.

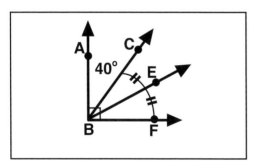

_____

_____

2. Find the measure of ∠TER. _____ Use complete sentences to explain your
    thinking.

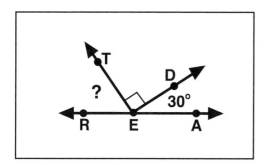

_____

_____

3. Find the measure of ∠ AXD if ∠ AXB = ∠ DXR. Circle the letter of the correct
    answer.

    a. 20 degrees
    b. 70 degrees
    c. 100 degrees
    d. 140 degrees

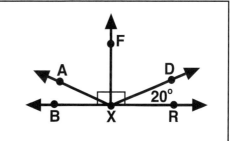

4. Find the measure of ∠ AXD if ∠ DXE is 80°.

    a. 20 degrees
    b. 70 degrees
    c. 100 degrees
    d. 140 degrees

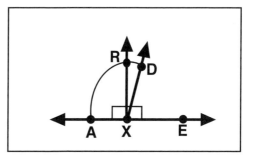

19—Trip to the Game

[1]Hannah and her younger brother Michael love sports. [2]Their favorite sports are football, tennis, and basketball. [3]Their Uncle Tom had season tickets to many games. [4]He told Hannah and Michael, "I will take you to any game you want if you do your homework every night." [5]Hannah and Michael said, "But we always do our homework!" [6]Uncle Tom was a math teacher, so he always wanted all the children in the family to work extra hard. [7]Uncle Tom said, "I want you to find out how much more in area a football field is than a college basketball court." [8]He added, "Remember that to find the area inside a rectangular shape, you multiply length times width."

[9]Hannah and Michael looked up the information at the library. [10]Knowing that Uncle Tom might ask them more questions in the future, Hannah wrote down the following information on a piece of paper.

Fact #1: Football field—360 feet by 160 feet

Fact #2: Tennis court—120 feet by 60 feet

Fact #3: College basketball court—94 feet by 50 feet

Source: http://www.infoplease.com/ipa/A0113430.html

Questions

1. Which of the following formulas can you use to find the area of a rectangle?

   a. Area = length + width

   b. Area = length x width

   c. Area = (2 x length) + (2 x width)

   d. Area = length x length, or length^2

   Give the number of the sentence that provides the best evidence for your answer. _____

2. Find the area of a football field. _____ Show your work.

Story, continued:

[11]When Uncle Tom came to visit again, Hannah and Michael had the right answer. [12]He was very proud of them. [13]But he added, "In football, a lot of measuring is done in yards. [14]Did you find the length of a football field in yards?" [15]Hannah and Michael said, "We just need a little time to figure that out."

[16]Later that day, Uncle Tom took Hannah and Michael to a basketball game.

[17]On the way to a basketball game, Hannah and Michael said to Uncle Tom, "Uncle Tom, we bet you don't know the perimeter of a tennis court." [18]Uncle Tom was surprised at their question. [19]"Hum, I'd have to look up the information. [20]I just can't remember." [21]Hannah and Michael said, "Ha, make sure you know that perimeter means to add all units along the outside border of a shape. [22]Uncle Tom laughed because, being a math teacher, he knew how to find the perimeter of any shape.

3. Find the area of a college basketball court. _____ Show your work.

4. How much bigger is the area of a football field compared to the area of a college basketball court? _____ Show your work.

5. Can you help Hannah and Michael find out how many yards long a football field is? _____ Show your work.

6. Find the perimeter of a tennis court. _____ Show your work.

    Give the number of the sentence that (along with the chart) provides the best evidence for your answer. _____

7. Without overlapping, about how many college basketball courts would fit inside one football field? _____ You may use your calculator to help you. Use complete sentences to explain your thinking.

    _____

    _____

20—The Perennial Garden

[1]Ms. Kamen wants to build a small perennial garden outside her classroom. [2]She wants to surround the outside edge of the garden with 24 feet of fence. [3]She wants her class to decide the area of the garden. [4]She tells them that she needs the garden to have a rectangular shape and reminds her students that the perimeter must be 24 feet. [5]She also reminds them that the garden can be in the shape of a square since a square is a rectangle. [6]She writes on the blackboard, "A square is a rectangle since it has 4 right angles." [7]Ms. Kamen tells her students to draw some designs and to use only whole number dimensions.

[8]Ami suggests that the garden should have the largest area possible so more perennials can be planted. [9]She has daisies, tulips, and daffodils she can bring from home. [10]She then draws a picture of her garden and shows it to the class. [11]Miguel looks at Ami's design and says that her garden would be too hard to weed, since getting to the center of Ami's garden would mean stepping on many flowers! [12]He draws a design with a width of 2 feet. [13]Scott agrees that Miguel's design would be better and adds that Miguel's design would have the same area as Ami's, since both have the same perimeter.

Questions

1. Can Ms. Kamen's garden be a circle? _____ Give the number the sentence which provides the best evidence for your answer. _____

2. Give the numbers of the two sentences that tell you what is meant by "perimeter." _____, _____ Define perimeter by using the information you've read above. Use a complete sentence.

   _____

   _____

3. Can the sides of Ms. Kamen's garden be fractions or decimals? _____ Give the number of the sentence that provides the best evidence for your answer. _____

4. Which of the following shapes is also considered a rectangle?

   a.   b.   c.   d.

   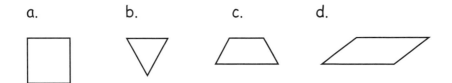

Give the numbers of the two sentences that provide the best evidence for your answer. _____, _____

5. a. On the following grid, draw all the possible rectangles that have a perimeter of 24 feet. Use 1 square to represent 1 square foot (Scale: 1 square = 1 square foot).

b. Find the area of each rectangle you drew above and write it inside each one.

6. What are the dimensions of Ami's design? _____ What is her area?_____ Give the number of the sentence that provides the best evidence for your answer. _____

7. What are the dimensions of Miguel's garden? _____ What is his area?_____ Give the number of the sentence that provides the best evidence for your answer. _____

8. Scott says that because Ami and Miguel's designs have the same perimeter, their areas are the same. Do you agree or disagree? Use complete sentences to explain your thinking.

_____

_____

9.   Miguel says that Ami's garden would be too hard to weed without stepping on many flowers. Do you agree? _____ Explain in complete sentences.

_____

_____

21—The Quadrilateral Factory

As you read this story, fill in the blanks of the Quadrilateral Family Picture (p. 49).

[1]In the Quadrilateral Factory, only four-sided polygons are made because that is what a quadrilateral is! [2]One day, the factory workers got tired of looking at the same old boring quadrilaterals and they decided to add a new ingredient to their machine. [3]They opened up a can with a label that read "Parallel." [4]They dumped the whole can into the quadrilateral machine. [5]To everyone's surprise, two shapes came out, each one with four sides, but—they were very different! [6]The factory workers named the first shape PARALLELOGRAM because it had both pairs of opposite sides parallel. [7]The other shape was very unusual! [8]They decided to name it TRAPEZOID because it had only two sides parallel. [9]They put this one on the shelf of an old cabinet.

[10]The factory workers decided to keep working on PARALLELOGRAM. [11]They opened up a can that read "Equal Sides" and put all of it into the machine. [12]The machine cranked and made strange noises. [13]Everyone waited quietly, and then a new shape came out. [14]Someone yelled, "This quadrilateral is a diamond. [15]We're rich!" [16]"No!," yelled someone else. [17]"It's not a diamond, it's just like PARALLELOGRAM but it has equal sides, so let's call it RHOMBUS." [18]And they all danced the rumba for a little while. [19]Then someone said, "I found a can that says 'Right Angles.'" [20]They took a parallelogram and added the entire can of "Right Angles" into the machine. [21]This new shape was a parallelogram, but all its angles were 90 degrees. [22]They named it RECTANGLE.

[23]One factory worker said, "This is magic! [24]Let's take a parallelogram and add a can of 'Equal Sides' and a can of 'Right Angles' and see what we get." [25]Another worker said, "That could be very risky!" [26]Some workers covered their eyes and some stood far away from the machine, afraid it might explode. [27]The machine made one loud sound and then began to play music as a beautiful shape came out. [28]All at once, everyone said, "Wow!" [29]This new shape was still a parallelogram, but it was truly amazing. [30]The worker who stood by the hot steamy machine said, "This shape is a rhombus because it has equal sides and that should be its name!" [31]"No, it's a rectangle because it has four right angles!" someone yelled louder. [32]"You're both right, it's a rhombus and a rectangle at the same time!" said the president of the company (her name was Ms. Math), "so I will name it SQUARE." [33]Then she said, "Good work! [34]Let's take pictures and tell the whole world that the first quadrilateral family has been born!"

[35]A factory worker whispered to a visitor, "A polygon is a many-sided closed shape where the sides are straight."

Quadrilateral Family Picture

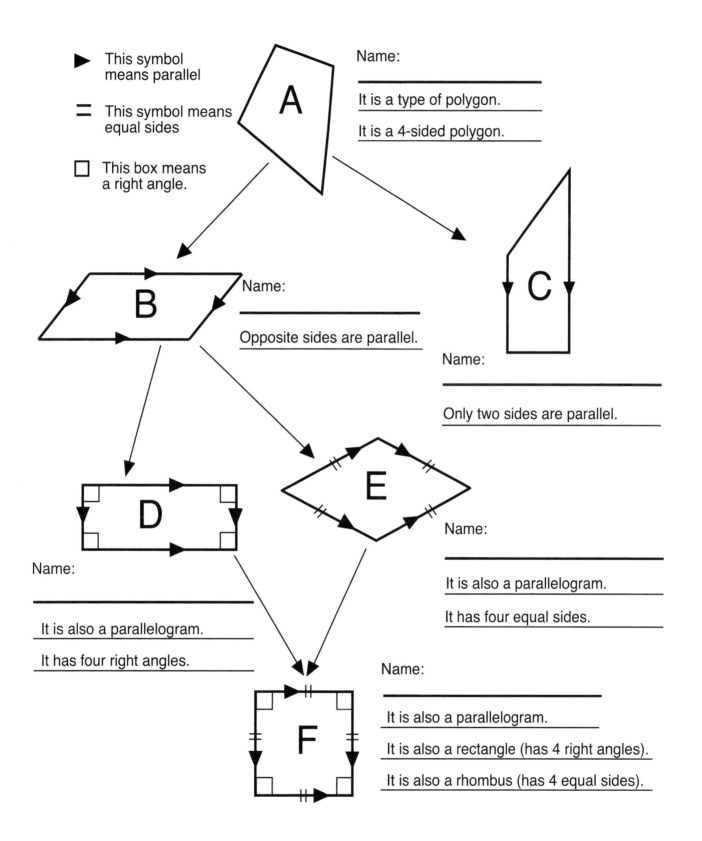

▶ This symbol means parallel

= This symbol means equal sides

☐ This box means a right angle.

A

Name:
_____

It is a type of polygon.

It is a 4-sided polygon.

B

Name:
_____

Opposite sides are parallel.

C

Name:
_____

Only two sides are parallel.

D

Name:
_____

It is also a parallelogram.

It has four right angles.

E

Name:
_____

It is also a parallelogram.

It has four equal sides.

F

Name:
_____

It is also a parallelogram.

It is also a rectangle (has 4 right angles).

It is also a rhombus (has 4 equal sides).

Questions

Did you remember to fill in the Quadrilateral Family Picture?

1. Of the following shapes, circle those that are NOT polygons.

| a. | b. | c. | d. |

Give the number of the sentence that provides the best evidence for your answer.
_____

2. Use a complete sentence to write a definition of a parallelogram. Use your definition to draw a picture.

_____

_____

Give the number of the sentence that provides the best evidence for your answer.
_____

3. Use a complete sentence to write a definition of a trapezoid. Use your definition to draw a picture of a trapezoid.

_____

_____

Give the number of the sentence that provides the best evidence for your answer.
_____

4. Is a rectangle a parallelogram? Use complete sentences to explain your thinking.

_____

_____

Give the numbers of the two sentences that provide the best evidence for your answer. _____, _____

5. Is a square a rectangle or a rhombus? Use complete sentences to explain your thinking.

_____

_____

Give the number of the sentence that provides the best evidence for your answer. _____

6. One of the workers made this conclusion: "A trapezoid is a parallelogram because it has many of the same properties." Give one reason to prove this worker is wrong. Use complete sentences to explain your thinking.

_____

_____

_____

22—The Toy Box Project

[1]Frank wanted to help his stepdad build a fancy toy box for Frank's little sister Melissa. [2]Frank's stepdad drew the basic designs A and B below. [3]Design C is a toy box that is being sold at the store.

[4]To build box A or box B it would cost Frank's stepdad about $237.00 in materials. [5]Frank thinks box B would have more volume or space for storage because it's taller. [6]Frank's stepdad could also buy toy box C at the store for $199.99. [7]He knows it would be cheaper to buy the store-bought toy box. [8]However, he is looking forward to spending time with Frank working on this project. [9]He wants Frank to paint the toy box purple, which is Melissa's favorite color. [10]To decide which box to build, he asks Frank to help him figure out the volume of each box. [11]Frank remembers that to find the volume of these toy boxes he has to multiply length times width times height.

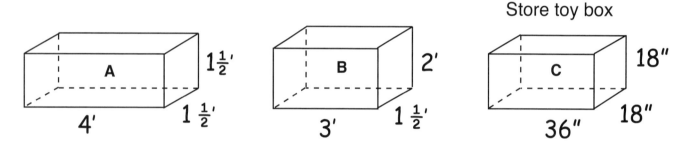

Store toy box

Questions

1. Compare the volume of box A with that of box B. Show your work.

   _____

   _____

2. Do you agree with Frank's statement that box B would fit more toys than box A because it's taller? Explain why or why not with a complete sentence.

   _____

   _____

3. Change each dimension on the store toy box to feet: 36" = _____feet, 18" = _____feet

4. Find the volume of the store toy box using your new dimensions. _____ Show your work.

5. If Frank's stepdad were to buy box C, would Melissa have more storage room for her toys than she would with the other boxes? Use complete sentences to explain your thinking.

   _____

   _____

6. About how much money would Frank's stepdad save if he bought the store toy box instead of building box A or B? _____ Show your work.

   Give the numbers of the two sentences that provide the best evidence for your answer. _____, _____

7. Which color has Frank chosen for Melissa's toy box?_____

   Give the number of the sentence that provides the best evidence for your answer. _____

8. Melissa has a doll that needs to lie flat in her toy box. The doll is $3\frac{1}{2}$ feet long. Which box should Frank and his stepdad choose for Melissa?_____ Explain in one sentence how you decided which box they should build.

   _____

   _____

9. Frank's stepdad decides to make the volume of Melissa's toy box 14 cubic feet. If he decides to keep the length 4' and the width 2', what will be the height of this new toy box? _____ Show your work.

23—The Case of the Missing Money

[1]Detective Jason found a note with some scribbled directions. [2]"This must be the clues to how to find the safe buried in the abandoned rectangular field!" said Detective Mara. [3]The note read, "Connect these points in order:

A (3,1), B (9,1), C (9,4), D (6,4), E (3,4), and A (3,1)." [4]Detective Jason began to draw the points on a grid. [5]Detective Mara said, "Remember, to get to Point A, you go over three units on the x-axis and then up 1 on the y-axis. [6]Make sure to label each point or you will get confused."

Questions

1. Draw and label the points on the grid below to help find the missing safe.

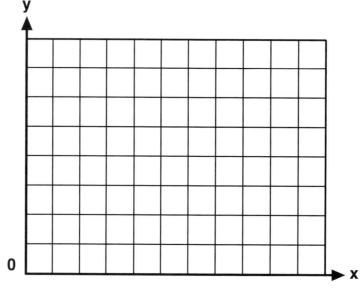

Story, continued:

[7]The second part of the note read, "Connect point A to point C. [8]Connect point A to point D and point D to point B. [9]Where segment DB intersects (meets) segment AC, that's where the safe is. [10]Now, to find the secret lock combination where I'm hiding the money, you will need to remember your math. [11]The first number is the area of shape ABCE. [12]The second number is the area of shape ABC. [13]The third number is three less than the area of shape ABD."

> To find the area of a triangle, find base times height then divide by 2. (Area = $\frac{1}{2}$ bh)

2. Where is the safe located? Mark an X on the spot and list the ordered pair. _____, _____

3. What shape is ABCE? _____ Why? Use complete sentences to explain your thinking.

    _____

    _____

4. What is the length of ABCE? _____ What is its width? _____

5. Find the area of shape ABCE. _____ Use complete sentences to explain your thinking.

    _____

6. What kinds of shapes are shapes ABC and ABD? Use complete sentences to explain your thinking.

    _____

7. Find the area of shape ABC. _____ Use complete sentences to explain your thinking.

    _____

    _____

8. Compare the base and the height of shapes ABC and ABD.

    _____

    _____

9. Why would shape ABC and shape ABD have the same area? Use complete sentences to explain your thinking.

    _____

    _____

10. What number is 3 less than the area of shape ABD? _____ Show your work.

11. Find the lock combination. _____ Give the numbers of the three sentences that provide the best evidence. _____, _____, _____

24—The Math Teachers' Room

[1]The math teachers were having a meeting in the Math Room. [2]The room had four mathematical sofas. [3]In the center of the room was a circle sofa. [4]The striped square sofa was on the right. [5]The white velvet right triangle sofa was on the left. [6]The checkered rectangle sofa was 10 feet by 4 feet. [7]The room was shaped as a square. [8]On the left wall hung a picture with some geometric formulas.

[9]Some of the math teachers became interested in all the shapes that were in the room. (It figures!) [10]Ms. Kamen, who ran the meeting, sat on the circle sofa. [11]She measured her sofa and found the radius to be 3 feet. [12]Mrs. Patterson, who sat on the striped square sofa, said, "I think this sofa has the largest area of all!" [13]Ms. Ged, who sat on the checkered rectangle sofa with Mr. Akins, was grading papers while she waited for the meeting to start. [14]Mrs. Colbert and Mrs. Hornbrook sat on the right triangle sofa and began to find its area. [15]They both thought their sofa was a lot bigger than the square sofa. [16]Mr. Bacon, who was looking out the window, said, "There are shapes everywhere, and that's what makes this world so beautiful!"

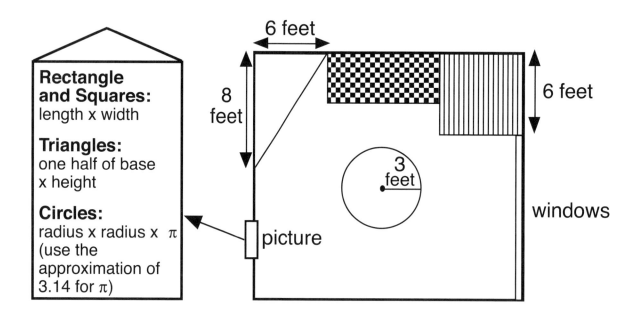

Rectangle and Squares: length x width

Triangles: one half of base x height

Circles: radius x radius x π (use the approximation of 3.14 for π)

6 feet

8 feet

6 feet

3 feet

picture

windows

Questions

1. What is the area of the sofa Ms. Ged and Mr. Akins are sitting on? Circle the letter of the correct answer.

   a. 12 square feet
   b. 40 square feet
   c. 20 square feet
   d. none of these

   Give the numbers of the two sentences that provide the best evidence for your answer. _____, _____

2. Find the area of the sofa that Mrs. Colbert and Mrs. Hornbrook are sitting on. _____ Show your work.

3. What is the area of the sofa that Mrs. Patterson is sitting on? Circle the letter of the correct answer.

   a. 6 square feet
   b. 18 square feet
   c. 24 square feet
   d. 36 square feet

4. Find the area of the sofa that Ms. Kamen is sitting on. _____ Show your work.

5. Which sofa has the largest area? Circle the letter of the correct answer.

   a. Mrs. Patterson's sofa
   b. the triangle sofa
   c. Ms. Kamen's sofa
   d. the rectangle sofa

6. What is the total length of the windows that extend from the couch to the corner of the room? _____ Use complete sentences to explain your thinking.

_____

_____

7. Find the area of the room. Use complete sentences to explain your thinking.

_____

_____

Give the number of the sentence that gives the best evidence to what shape the room is. _____

IV
PROBABILITY

25—Sum of Six

[1]Ami and Miguel played a dice game. [2]They took turns tossing two six-sided dice and found the sum.

[3]They played a total of 30 times. [4]Ami graphed the results below.

Sum of Two Dice

Sum	Tally
2	X
3	X X
4	X X X
5	X X X
6	X X X X
7	X X X X X
8	X X X X X X
9	X X X
10	X X
11	X
12	

Questions

1. How come Ami and Miguel did not get any sums of 1 or 13 when they rolled two six-sided dice? (Circle the letter of the correct choice.)

   a. They were not lucky enough.

   b. Not many combinations add up to 1 or 13.

   c. It is not possible to get a 1 or a 13.

   d. None of the above.

2. Of the possible sums, which three did they get least often? _____ Why do you think that is? Use complete sentences to explain your thinking.

   _____

   _____

3. List all the possible ways of getting a sum of 7 and all the ways of getting a sum of 8.

   Sum of 7   Sum of 8

4. Why do you think 6, 7, and 8 were the most frequently found sums in Amy and Miguel's game? Use complete sentences to explain your thinking.

   _____

   _____

5. How many different outcomes are there when playing this game? (Consider getting 2 and then 3 as different from getting 3 and then 2). Circle the letter of the correct answer.

   a. 9
   b. 10
   c. 12
   d. 36

6.   a. You need two dice. Roll both dice and add the results. Do this 30 times. Mark each sum with an X on the grid below. After you are done, turn your paper sideways (counterclockwise) and you will see that you made a bar graph!

   b. Compare your results with Ami and Miguel's results. What is similar and different when you compare both graphs? Use complete sentences.

   _____

   _____

   _____

Sum

2											
3											
4											
5											
6											
7											
8											
9											
10											
11											
12											

26—The Buttons

[1]Veni's mom had a jar with some old buttons in it. [2]She asked Veni to pick two buttons for a blouse she was making Veni for the school musical. [3]Veni began to make a list of how many buttons of each color were in the jar. [4]Her mother said, "I know that I have twice as many red buttons as yellow buttons and half as many purple buttons as yellow buttons."

[5]Veni counted the buttons anyway and agreed that her mother was right. [6]Yet she couldn't decide on which buttons to pick, so she put them all back in the jar and shook the jar.

[7]She said to her mom, "I'll just take a chance and reach in without looking and pick two buttons, one at a time. [8]I'll probably get two red buttons if I pick them at random since there are a lot of red buttons." [9]Her mom said, "Well, your blouse would still look nice even if you ended up with two different colored buttons." [10]Below is the chart that Veni started to make.

red	
blue	8
yellow	6
purple	

Questions

1. Before Veni picked any buttons from the jar, how many buttons were red? _____

   Give the number of the sentence that provides the best evidence for your answer. _____

2. Before Veni picked any buttons from the jar, how many were purple? _____

   Give the number of the sentence that provides the best evidence for your answer. _____

3. Complete Veni's chart above. How many buttons are in the jar? _____

4. If Veni reaches into the jar without looking, what is the probability that she will pick a red button? Circle the letter of the best answer.

   a. $\frac{8}{29}$

   b. $\frac{3}{29}$

   c. $\frac{12}{29}$

   d. $\frac{1}{12}$

5. If Veni reaches into the jar without looking, what is the probability that she will pick a purple button? Circle the letter of the best answer.

   a. $\frac{8}{29}$

   b. $\frac{3}{29}$

   c. $\frac{12}{29}$

   d. none

6. Veni reached into the jar without looking and her first button was a red button. She gave the red button to her mom, who sewed it on her blouse. If Veni shakes the jar again and reaches without looking, what is the probability that she will get another red button? Use complete sentences to explain your thinking.

   _____

   _____

   _____

27—The Spinner Game

¹Daria and Juan decide to play with some spinners that Juan's grandfather still kept from when he was a child. ²Juan said to Daria, "If you land on an even number, you get 2 points. ³If you land on an odd number, you lose 1 point. ⁴If I land on an odd number, I get 2 points. ⁵If I land on an even number, I lose 1 point." ⁶Daria reminded Juan that all even numbers can be divided by two without a remainder. ⁷Juan and Daria played the game for ten turns.

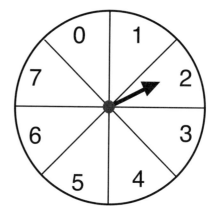

Questions

1. How many points does Juan get or lose if he lands on "5"?_____ Give the number of the sentence that provides the best evidence for your answer. _____

2. How many points does Daria get or lose if she lands on "5"? _____ Give the number of the sentence that provides the best evidence for your answer. _____

3. Does Daria get or lose points if she lands on "0"?_____ Divide 0 by 2 to show if it's even or odd. Show your work. Is 0 even or odd? _____

    Give the number of the sentence that provides the best evidence to call 0 even or odd. _____

4. Juan got these numbers on his ten turns: 6, 6, 1, 3, 0, 4, 2, 3, 4, 6. What is Juan's score? _____ Show your work.

5. Daria got these numbers on her ten turns: 0, 3, 4, 4, 7, 5, 0, 3, 1, 7. What is Daria's score? _____Show your work.

6. What were Juan's chances of winning two points? _____

7. What were Juan's chances of losing one point? _____

8. What were Daria's chances of winning two points? _____

9. What were Daria's chances of losing one point? _____

10. Do you think this is a fair game? Use complete sentences to explain your thinking.

    _____

    _____

Story, continued:

[8]Juan decided to show Daria another spinner game. [9]He told Daria, "I have a different spinner, and this time if I land on a prime number I get 3 points. [10]If you land on a composite number, you get 3 points." [11]Daria asked, "Do any of us lose points this time?" [12]Juan answered, "No, we don't lose any points." [13]Juan showed Daria the new spinner shown below.

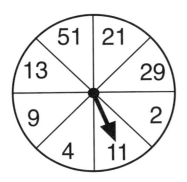

[14]Daria looked at the spinner and said, "Not fair—there are more prime numbers on this spinner than composite numbers, so your chances of winning are better!" [15]Juan wasn't sure Daria was right, so they both looked up the definition of a prime number in their math book. [16]Juan read from his math book, "A prime number is any whole number larger than 1 which has only two factors. [17]Numbers larger than 1 which are not prime are called 'composite.'" [18]Daria was not convinced because she believed that 51 was prime. [19]Juan divided 51 by a number other than 51 or 1, and Daria decided to play the game for five turns each.

11. Give the number of the sentence that tells you what Juan would get if there were a 7 and he landed on it. _____ How many points would he get? _____

12. Give the number of the sentence that tells you what Daria would get if she landed on a 4. _____ How many points would she get? _____

13. Explain how you would find out if 9 is a prime number or not. Use complete sentences to explain your thinking.

_____

_____

14. Why was Daria so concerned about 51 being a prime or not? Use complete sentences to explain your thinking.

_____

_____

15. Tell what Juan might have done exactly to convince Daria to play the game. Use complete sentences to explain your thinking.

_____

_____

16. These were the numbers Juan got: 51, 2, 11, 9, 4 and these are the numbers Daria got: 9, 4, 4, 2, 51. Who won the game? _____ Show your work.

Play the Spinner Game

Cut out the spinner circle and the pointer. Trace the pointer on a piece of cardboard and cut it out. Attach it to the center of the spinner circle with a paper fastener. You can also use a partially straightened paper clip as the pointer, and hold it with a pencil.

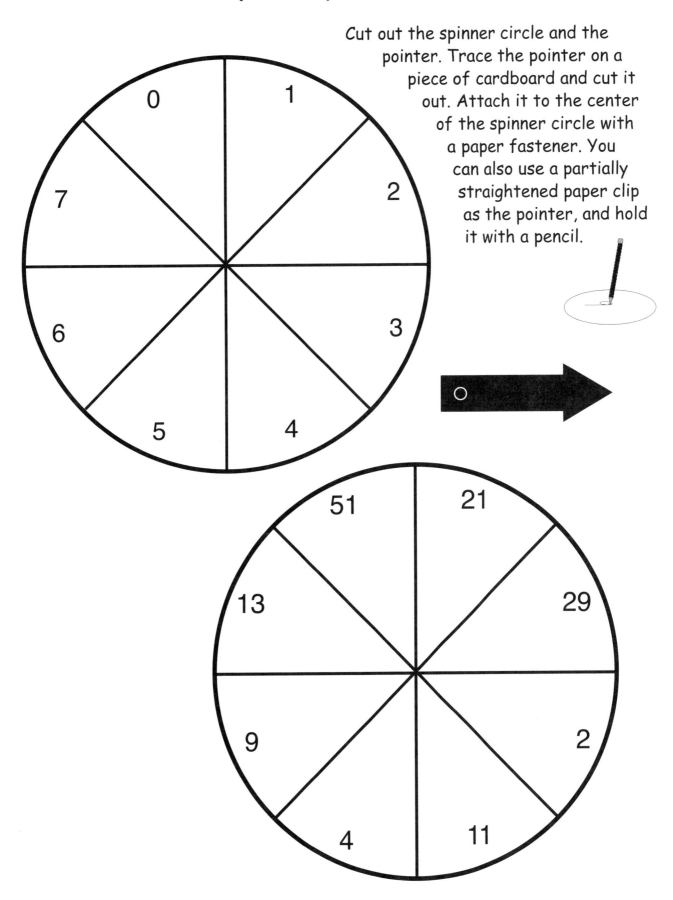

28—The Game of Dish

[1]Native Americans played many games of chance. [2]The Cayuga Indians from upstate New York played a game called the Game of Dish. [3]They used a wooden bowl and six peach stones. [4]The Cayuga Indians made one side of each stone darker by burning it. [5]The other side was white. [6]To play the game they would put the six stones in the bowl and shake it. [7]If all the stones landed with the same color up (all black or all white) then the player got five points. [8]If a player got five stones of one color and one of a different color (5 white and 1 black or 5 black and 1 white) then the player got only one point. [9]Any other outcomes* or results got no points.

*An outcome is what can happen or what you get during your turn.

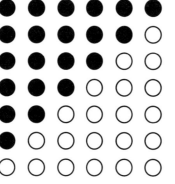

Points

_____

_____

_____

_____

_____

_____

Questions

1. Which of the following conclusions is false?_____

   a. A player must score 2 points in one turn in this game.

   b. There were 6 playing pieces in this game.

   c. A player could score 5 points in one of her turns.

   d. The Cayuga Indians were from upstate New York.

   Give the number of the sentence that provides the best evidence for your answer.

   _____

2. What are two ways a player can reach 6 points in this game? Use complete sentences to explain your thinking.

_____

_____

3. Write the number of points a player would get for each of these outcomes. Then figure out the player's final score.

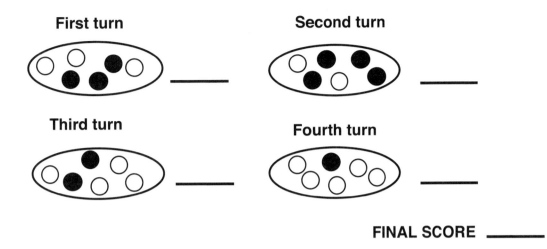

First turn _____

Second turn _____

Third turn _____

Fourth turn _____

FINAL SCORE _____

4. Why do you think the Cayuga Indians decided to give points as they did (five points for getting all six stones with the same color, only one point for five stones of the same color and one of a different color, and no points for any other results)? Use complete sentences to explain your thinking.

_____

_____

_____

_____

The Game of Dish Scoring Sheet

Play the Dish Game with only three seeds. You can use lima beans, for example. Just color one side black on each lima bean. You get 8 points if you get all three lima beans of the same color (all three black or all three neutral). You get 4 points for two of the same color. Play this game with a friend at least ten times each.

Number of Tries

Name	1	2	3	4	5	6	7	8	9	10	Total

Number of Tries

Name	1	2	3	4	5	6	7	8	9	10

Number of Tries

Name	1	2	3	4	5	6	7	8	9	10

Number of Tries

Name	1	2	3	4	5	6	7	8	9	10

29—The Breakfast Special

¹It was Sunday. ²Josie, her brother Hector, and Mr. and Mrs. Cavallo took Grandma Cavallo out to breakfast. ³The restaurant had a special for $3.99 every Sunday. ⁴To get the special, you have to pick one main dish and one side dish. ⁵Grandma Cavallo does not eat eggs or sausage. ⁶Josie hates sausage. ⁷The Cavallo family ordered the breakfast special for each member of their family.

Main Dishes	Side Dishes
Scrambled Eggs with Toast	Bacon
Pancakes	Sausage
Waffles	

Questions

1. Write down the different meals that Grandma Cavallo could have chosen.

   Give the number of the sentence that provides the best evidence that Grandma Cavallo did not choose scrambled eggs with her meal. _____

2. What is the probability that Grandma Cavallo will eat waffles and bacon? _____ Use complete sentences to explain your thinking.

   _____

   _____

3. Write down all the different meals that Josie would likely choose.

   Give the number of the sentence that provides the best evidence that Josie did not choose waffles with sausage. _____

4. a. Describe all the different meals that Hector could choose.

   b. How many different meal choices does Hector have? _____

5. What is the probability that Hector will choose pancakes and sausage? _____

6. 🔺 Is it possible for everyone in the Cavallo family to eat a different meal?
   _____ Provide the evidence to your answer by showing an example of what each
   person could eat, making sure that no two people eat the same things.

   Josie
   _____

   Hector
   _____

   Grandma
   _____

   Mrs. Cavallo
   _____

   Mr. Cavallo
   _____

7. 🔺 A family of seven shows up at the restaurant and wants to order the $3.99
   special for each person in their family. Is it possible for each one to order a
   different meal? _____Use complete sentences to explain your thinking.

   _____

   _____

   _____

V
STATISTICS

30—The Great Goldfish Giveaway

[1]A pet store was planning to give away two goldfish to each person who walked through its door each hour on the hour. [2]The owner graphed the results below. [3]She had 200 goldfish to give away for the whole day.

[4]At 11 a.m., she got nervous that she might not have enough goldfish for the whole day. [5]Next door, a popular restaurant had a sign that read, "Lunch Special at Noon: Two people eat for the price of one."

Goldfish Winners

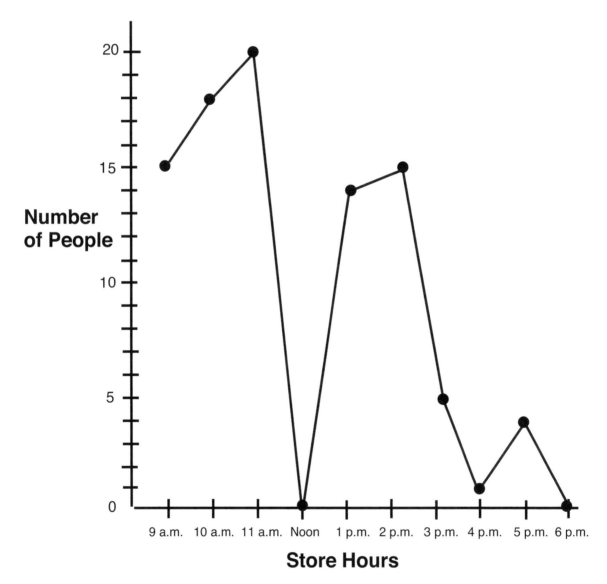

Number of People

Store Hours

Questions

1. How many goldfish were given away at 10 a.m.? _____ Give the number of the sentence that provides the best evidence for your answer. _____ Circle the dot in the graph that shows the evidence for your answer.

2. How many more goldfish were given away before noon than in the afternoon? Circle the letter of the correct answer.

    a. 38
    b. 30
    c. 100
    d. 28

3. How many goldfish were given away all day? _____ Show your work.

4. Did the owner have enough goldfish for the entire day? _____ Explain with a complete sentence.

    _____

    _____

5. How many goldfish were left over, if any? Circle the letter of the correct answer.

    a. 8
    b. 10
    c. 16
    d. 0

6. At 11 a.m., why did the owner get nervous that she might not have enough goldfish to give away? Use complete sentences to explain your thinking.

    _____

    _____

    _____

7. What might be a reason that no one came into the store at noon? Explain in complete sentences.

    _____

    _____

    _____

    Give the number of the sentence that provides the best evidence for your answer. _____

31—Jameel's Math Scores

[1]Jameel graphed his first five tests in his math class. [2]All his scores so far are multiples of 5. [3]Help Jameel find his mean (or average) score. [4]The mean is the result of adding all scores and dividing by the number of scores.

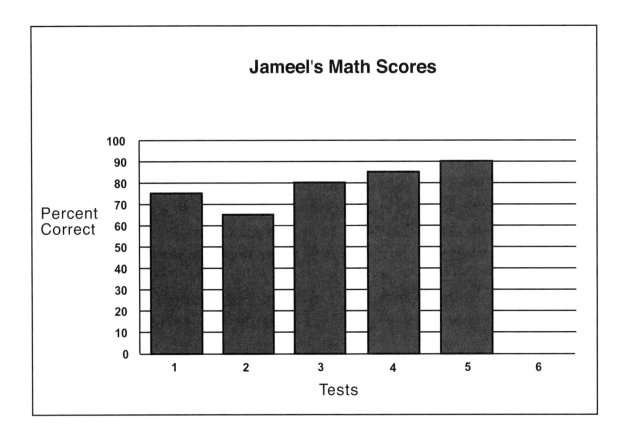

Questions

1. What does the vertical axis on the graph represent? Use a complete sentence to explain your thinking.

_____

_____

2. What does the horizontal axis on the graph represent? Use a complete sentence to explain your thinking.

_____

_____

3. Is Jameel's first score a 76 or a 75? _____
   Give the number of the sentence that provides the best evidence for your answer. _____

4. What are the scores on Jameel's first five tests?

_____

_____

5. What is Jameel's mean score after his fifth test? _____ Show your work.

Give the number of the sentence that best helps you find the answer. _____

6. Just by looking at Jameel's first five scores, can you predict what Jameel's sixth score might be? _____ Why or why not? Use complete sentences to explain your thinking.

_____

_____

_____

7. If Jameel got an 85 on his sixth test, what would his new mean score be? _____ Show your work.

8. By how much did his mean score change? _____

9. Amanda got these scores on her first five math tests: 70, 80, 68, 80, and 85. After her sixth test, she had the same mean score that Jameel had after he got an 85 on his sixth test. What score did Amanda get on her sixth test? _____ Show your work.

10. On the grid on the next page, graph Amanda's test scores. Don't forget to put a title on your graph and label each axis correctly.

32—Cody's Homework Graph

[1]Cody's dad started a graph of the number of minutes Cody spent doing homework from Monday through Friday. [2]His dad promised Cody that he would get a little gift if he spent more than 3 hours on homework during that week. [3]One day early in the week, Cody spent a total of one half-hour doing his science homework. [4]Another day Cody spent a total of 1 hour and 20 minutes on homework when he tried to finish a math poster the night before it was due. [5]He just kept putting it off and putting it off, even though he knew for two weeks that it was due on Friday, September 28th. [6]On each of the other two days, he spent equal amounts of time reading his social studies book.

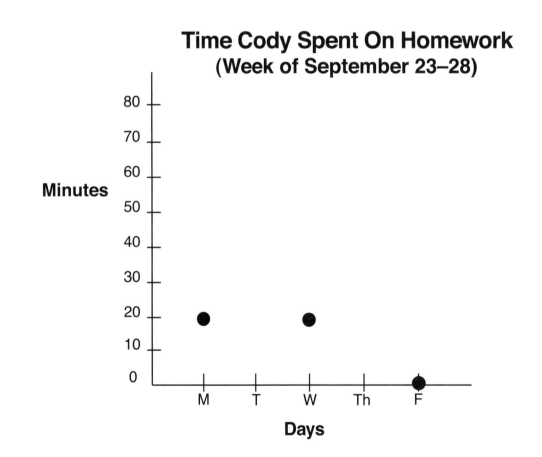

Time Cody Spent On Homework
(Week of September 23–28)

Minutes

Days

Questions

1. Complete the line graph above.

2. On which day of the week did Cody spend time doing his science homework?
   _____

   Give the number of the sentence that provides the best evidence for your answer.
   _____

3. On which day did Cody work on his poster? _____

    Give the numbers of the two sentences that provide the best evidence for your answer. _____, _____

4. Of the days he spent reading social studies, how many minutes per day did Cody spend reading his social studies book?_____ Use complete sentences to explain your thinking.

    _____

    _____

5. How much more time did Cody spend on his math poster than on science homework? _____ Show your work.

6. Did Cody get a little gift from his dad that week? Use complete sentences to explain your thinking.

    _____

    _____

    Give the number of the sentence that provides the best evidence for your answer. _____

33—Temperature Tale of Two Cities

Temperatures in Boston & Miami

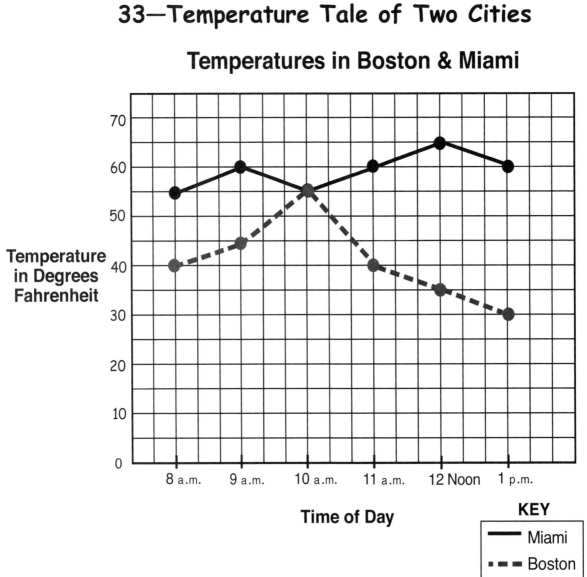

Temperature in Degrees Fahrenheit

Time of Day

KEY
—— Miami
∎ ∎ ∎ Boston

Questions

1. Study the graph above and fill out the temperature charts below:

Boston

Time	Temperature
8 a.m.	
9 a.m.	
10 a.m.	
11 a.m.	
12 Noon	
1 p.m.	

Miami

Time	Temperature
8 a.m.	
9 a.m.	
10 a.m.	
11 a.m.	
12 Noon	
1 p.m.	

2. What was the difference in temperature between the two cities at 8 a.m.? _____
    Show your work.

3. Which of the two cities showed the bigger rise in temperature from one hour to
    the next?_____

    Use a complete sentence to explain your thinking.

    _____

    _____

4. At what time of the day did the two cities have the same temperature? _____Use
    a complete sentence to explain your thinking.

    _____

    _____

5. During what time of the day was the temperature in both cities going down? Use a
    complete sentence to write your answer.

    _____

6. Find the mean (average) temperature for Miami for the six hours shown on the
    graph. Round your answer to the nearest whole number. _____ Show your work.

7. Find the mean (average) temperature for Boston for the six hours shown on the
    graph. Round your answer to the nearest whole number. _____ Show your work.

34—Making Money Mowing

[1]Irina made a total of $100 one month mowing lawns in her neighborhood. [2]She spent $\frac{1}{10}$ of the total on a gift for her grandfather's birthday. [3]She spent $\frac{1}{5}$ of the total on a T-shirt for her little brother. [4]She spent $\frac{1}{4}$ of the total on a new video game. [5]She also spent some money at the movies. [6]She saved the rest of the money. [7]Irina made the following chart to keep track of her money.

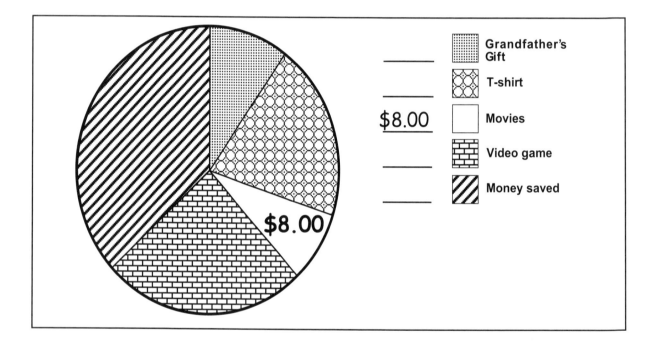

Legend:
- Grandfather's Gift
- $8.00 — T-shirt
- Movies
- Video game
- Money saved

$8.00

Questions

1. By just looking at the pie chart above, can you show the items Irina spent money on, in order from least spent to most?

   She used the least for _____

   She used more for _____

   She used more for _____

   She used more for _____

   She used most for _____

2. How much money did Irina spend on her grandfather's gift? _____ Show your work.

    Give the number of the sentence that provides the best evidence for your answer. _____

3. How much money did Irina spend on the T-shirt? _____ Show your work.

    Give the number of the sentence that provides the best evidence for your answer. _____

4. Without doing any arithmetic, how can you find out which two expenses added together come the closest to $50? Use complete sentences to explain your thinking. Use the chart to help you.

    _____

    _____

    _____

5. How much did Irina spend altogether? _____ Show your work and label each amount in the blanks on the chart.

6. How much of the total did Irina save? _____ Show your work. Give the number of the sentence that provides the best evidence for your answer. _____

7. What percent of the total did Irina spend on her grandfather's gift? _____ Remember to change her fraction to $\frac{?}{100}$ to find the percent. Show your work.

8. What percent of the total money earned did Irina spend altogether? _____
   Show your work.

9. Circle the letter of the best title for the circle graph. Write the title on top of
   the graph.

   a. How Irina Spent All Her Money

   b. How Irina Saved Her Summer Money

   c. What Irina Did to Earn Her $100

   d. What Irina Did With Her $100

10. The whole circle represents the total amount of money earned by Irina. A
    circle has 360 degrees. How many degrees are taken up by the section that shows
    what Irina spent on her grandfather? _____

35—The World Record Fish Report

[1]Ms. Kamen asked her students to write a report on their favorite hobby. [2]Tabitha loves to fish. [3]She decided to write a report on the largest fish ever caught. [4]Tabitha also wanted to make a large poster chart of her data. [5]Below is the data that Tabitha found on the Internet for some of her favorite fish.

Freshwater (Lakes & Rivers) World Records

Carp	75 lbs 11 oz	1987	France
Chinook Salmon	97 lbs 4 oz	1985	Arkansas, USA
Coho Salmon	33 lbs 4 oz	1989	New York State, USA
Largemouth Bass	22 lbs 4 oz	1932	Georgia, USA
Rainbow Trout	42 lbs 2 oz	1970	Arkansas, USA
Sharptoothed Catfish	79 lbs 5 oz	1992	South Africa
White Sturgeon[*]	468 lbs	1983	California, USA

* largest freshwater fish ever caught

From: http://www.schooloflyfishing.com/resources/worldfreshrecords.htm

Saltwater (Ocean) World Records

Atlantic Halibut	255 lbs 4 oz	1989	Massachusetts, USA
Atlantic Sailfish	141 lbs	1994	Angola
Bluefin Tuna	1,496 lbs	1979	Nova Scotia
Great White Shark[*]	2,664 lbs	1959	Australia
Pacific Blue Marlin	1,376 lbs	1982	Hawaii, USA
Pacific Sailfish	221 lbs	1947	Ecuador
Swordfish	1,182 lbs	1953	Chile

* largest saltwater fish ever caught

From: http://www.schooloflyfishing.com/resources/worldsaltrecords.htm

Questions

1. How much heavier is the largest saltwater fish ever caught compared to the largest freshwater fish ever caught? _____ Show your work.

2. Based on the information that Tabitha found, what does NOT seem to be true? Circle the letter of the best answer.

   a. Blue marlins are bigger than sailfish.
   b. Big fish can be found in both the ocean and fresh water.
   c. Bluefin tuna are the biggest animals in the ocean.
   d. World record fish have come from all over the world.

   Use complete sentences to explain your thinking. Provide evidence from the chart to support your answer.

   _____

   _____

3. How many ounces is the world record sharptoothed catfish? _____ (Remember that 1 pound = 16 ounces.) Show your work.

Story, continued:

⁶Ms. Kamen asked Tabitha to choose only one type of fish to talk about in her oral report. ⁷Tabitha chose the shark and did more research. ⁸She made a list of the largest sharks ever caught. ⁹She brought a poster for the class to fill out after she read her report. ¹⁰This is Tabitha's report:

¹¹"My report is on sharks. ¹²You're not going to believe how big some sharks get. ¹³There may be bigger sharks in the ocean, but these are the biggest sharks ever caught. ¹⁴As I read this information, listen carefully so we can fill out this poster for our classroom." ¹⁵Tabitha went on to say, "The biggest blue shark ever caught was 454 lbs. ¹⁶It was caught in Martha's Vineyard, Massachusetts, in 1996. ¹⁷You think that's big? ¹⁸The biggest shark ever caught was a great white shark. ¹⁹It was 2,210 pounds more than that. ²⁰This great white shark was caught off the southern coast of Australia in 1959. ²¹Hammerhead sharks are really cool. ²²The biggest hammerhead shark ever caught was 1673 pounds less than the world record great white shark. ²³It was caught in Sarasota, Florida, in 1982. ²⁴Another very large shark caught off the coast of South Carolina was a tiger shark. ²⁵It holds the record for tiger sharks, at 1780 lbs. ²⁶It was caught five years after the largest great white shark ever caught. ²⁷The last shark on my chart is the shortfin mako shark. ²⁸It was caught in Black River, Mauritius, in 1988. ²⁹To find its weight, multiply the weight of the blue shark by 3 and subtract 247 pounds!"

4. Based on Tabitha's report, fill out the World Record Shark Poster on the next page. You may use this space to do the math required.

The World Record Shark Poster

Type of Shark	Weight in Pounds	Where Caught	Date Caught
Blue			
			1982
		Black River, Mauritius*	
	1,780 lbs		
Great White			

*Mauritius is an island in the Indian Ocean, surrounded by coral reefs. It's about 1,250 miles from the African coast.

VI
PRE-ALGEBRA

36—The King Orders the Operations!

[1]The king and queen announced the new rules for the Math Kingdom. [2]The four knights—Division, Multiplication, Addition, and Subtraction—were called to hear the new rules. [3]The king said, "You are the operation knights, for you always get numbers to operate or work with one another. [4]Starting today there will be no more confusion as to who operates first. [5]Too many people in the kingdom are getting the wrong answer!" he screamed. [6]The king then called up Division and Multiplication to the throne and said, "Both of you will now be most important. [7]When numbers are lined up, Division and Multiplication will always do their jobs first, from left to right." [8]All the numbers, the common people of the kingdom, and the shapes listened quietly. [9]Multiplication asked, "Will I go first from now on? [10]My dear Aunt Sally told me so!" [11]The king said, "No, no, don't be greedy! [12]You and Division will have the same rank. [13]Whichever one of you stands first in order from left to right will operate first. [14]Then, after both of you are done, Addition and Subtraction,

or Subtraction and Addition, will operate next also from left to right." [15]The queen added, "These will be the new rules from now on, unless I decide to throw parentheses around you, in which case, whoever is in the parentheses will work first!"

[16]The king asked some numbers and operations to come up front and they lined up this way: 15 ÷ 5 x 3 + 8

[17]The king asked Duke Square, Dutchess Trapezoid and Lady Circle, who was eating a big π, to see if they understood the new rules. [18]Duke Square said the answer was 9. [19]Duchess Trapezoid said her hips hurt and she did not want to answer. [20]Lady Circle, with a mouthful, said "17". [21]The king said, "Roll over here, Lady Circle." [22]All of the numbers that were present (some were in Hotel Infinity) held their breath. [23]No one knew if Lady Circle was in trouble for getting the wrong answer. [24]Maybe she was in trouble for eating in the court. [25]Or was the king calling her over because she had the right answer?

Questions

1. What are addition, subtraction, multiplication, and division called in math?
   a. operations
   b. symbols
   c. facts
   d. Knights of the Round Table

2. Why did the king feel that rules were necessary? Use complete sentences to explain your thinking.

_____

_____

_____

Give the numbers of the two sentences that provide the best evidence for your answer. _____, _____

3. When multiplication and division are the only operations in a problem that has no parentheses, do you have to multiply first? _____ Give the number of the sentence that provides the best evidence for your answer. _____

4. When addition and subtraction are the only operations in a problem that has no parentheses, do you have to add first? _____ Give the number of the sentence that provides the best evidence for your answer. _____

5. What would be the ending that best fits this story?

   a. Lady Circle was sent to prison for eating in court and getting the wrong answer.

   b. A ball was held in Duke Square's honor for getting the right answer.

   c. Lady Circle was praised for getting the correct answer and was made Queen of a new kingdom called the PI kingdom.

   d. None of them got the right answer and the king became enraged.

6. Find the answer to the problem below. _____ Give the number of the sentence which provides the best evidence to how to start the problem. _____ Explain in one or two sentences the steps that you followed to get your answer.

$$15 \div 5 \times (3 + 8)$$

_____

_____

_____

37—Symbol Says...

[1]Ms. Kamen had a new game she wanted her students to play. [2]She gave everyone a number. [3]Some numbers were whole numbers, and some were fractions. [4]Luis had the fraction $\frac{1}{3}$. [5]Eddy had the whole number 4. [6]Amanda had the fraction $\frac{1}{2}$. [7]Daria got a letter "y" instead of a specific number. [8]When Daria saw that she had a "y" she asked, "But, Ms. Kamen, I don't know what to do with this 'y.'" [9]Ms. Kamen replied, "Daria, 'y' is a variable that means you can let it be any number you want!" [10]Eddy became very upset and said, "That's not fair. [11]I want to choose any number I want, too." [12]Ms. Kamen explained to the class that everyone would switch their numbers on the second round.

[13]Then Ms. Kamen went on to say, "When I hold up one of these cards—the star, the sun, the planet, or the comet—you will do what it says on the board next to the card." [14]Here is what was on the board:

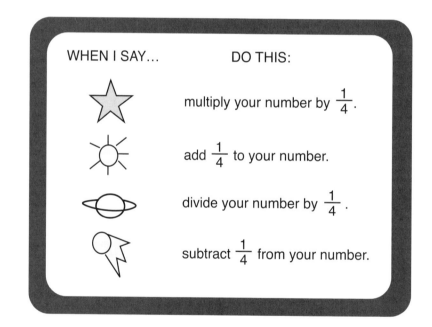

WHEN I SAY...	DO THIS:
★	multiply your number by $\frac{1}{4}$.
☀	add $\frac{1}{4}$ to your number.
♄	divide your number by $\frac{1}{4}$.
☄	subtract $\frac{1}{4}$ from your number.

Questions

1. When Ms. Kamen said, "Symbol says STAR your number," what should Eddy and Luis have gotten for their answers? Show your work.

   Eddy should have gotten _____. Luis should have gotten _____.

2.   When Ms. Kamen said, "Symbol says PLANET your number," what should Eddy and Luis have gotten for their answers? Show your work.

Eddy should have gotten _____. Luis should have gotten _____.

3.   When Ms. Kamen said, "Symbol says COMET your number," what should Eddy and Amanda have gotten for their answers? Show your work.

Eddy should have gotten _____. Amanda should have gotten _____.

4.   When Ms. Kamen said, "Symbol says SUN your number," what should Eddy and Luis have gotten for their answers? Show your work.

Eddy should have gotten _____. Luis should have gotten _____.

5.   Each time that Ms. Kamen said STAR, PLANET, COMET, or SUN, Daria let her "y" be the number 1 because she thought that would be the easiest number. What answers should she have gotten? Show your work.

For STAR she should have gotten _____. For PLANET she should have gotten _____. For COMET she should have gotten _____. For SUN she should have gotten _____.

6.   When Eddy got a turn at having the letter "y," he let his "y" be the number zero each time. What should Eddy have gotten when Ms. Kamen said, "Symbol says PLANET your number"? _____ Use a complete sentence to explain your thinking.

_____

_____

38—The Case of the Missing Numbers

[1]Ms. Kamen has an envelope with these whole numbers in it. [2]She asked her students to try each number in each of the inequalities below.

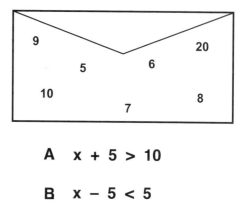

A   **x + 5 > 10**

B   **x − 5 < 5**

Questions

1. Which numbers in Ms. Kamen's envelope, when substituting for x, make inequality A true? _____

2. The number 5 does not make the inequality A true. Why not? Use complete sentences to explain your thinking.

   _____

   _____

3. What numbers in the envelope make inequality B true?_____

4. The number 10 does not make the inequality B true. Why not? Use complete sentences to explain your thinking.

   _____

   _____

5. What numbers work in both inequalities?_____

Story, continued:

[3]Ms. Kamen told her class that there were many other numbers beside whole numbers that made both inequalities true. [4]She showed her class all the positive numbers that work for inequality A by graphing these numbers on a number line.

[5]She explained that an open circle on the number 5 means that 5 does not make the inequality A true. [6]All the numbers that are shaded to the right do. [7]She also darkened the arrowhead to show that all the numbers to the right of 11 also make inequality A true.

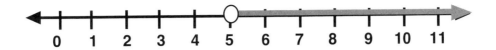

Look at the graph Ms. Kamen drew above.

6. Does the number $6\frac{1}{2}$ make inequality A true? _____ Use a complete sentence to explain your thinking.

_____

_____

7. Does the number 48 make inequality A true? Use a complete sentence to explain your thinking.

_____

_____

8. What does an open circle on a number line mean? Use a complete sentence to explain your thinking.

_____

_____

Give the number of the sentence that provides the best evidence for your answer.
_____

9. What does a darkened arrowhead on the number line mean? Use a complete sentence to explain your thinking.

_____

_____

10. Using the graph below, graph all the numbers (not just whole numbers) that make inequality B (x – 5 < 5) true.

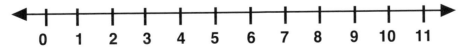

11. Look at Ms. Kamen's graph and look at your graph. Between what two numbers are ALL the numbers that make both inequalities true? _____

39—The Busy Elevator

[1]A company owns a five-story building. [2]The building has three floors under the main floor, as shown above. [3]The building has an elevator that is always busy. [4]Mr. Garcia, Ms. Long, Mr. Keyes, Mrs. Singer, Mrs. Ezra, and Dr. Du are all on their way to a different meeting. [5]One of these people is the president of the company. [6]Following are the meetings that are taking place on these floors. [7]On the Basement floor (-1), there is a computer meeting. [8]On the Sub-basement floor (-2), there is a meeting about a new product the company is making. [9]On Floor 1, there is a meeting to create more ads for TV. [10]On Floor 2, there is a lunch meeting in the cafeteria with new employees. [11]On Floor 3, there is a meeting to talk about how much money the company is making. [12]On Floor 4, there is a meeting to give the new president of the company an award.

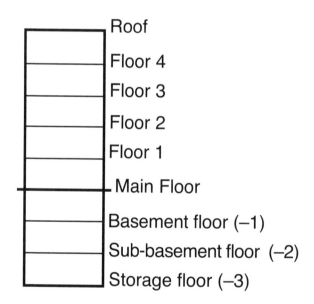

Roof
Floor 4
Floor 3
Floor 2
Floor 1
Main Floor
Basement floor (−1)
Sub-basement floor (−2)
Storage floor (−3)

Questions

1. Dr. Du takes the elevator from the Sub-basement floor and goes up four floors to his meeting. Which meeting is he going to? _____

   Give the number of the sentence that provides the best evidence for your answer. _____

   Complete this equation to show what the elevator did: -2 + 4 = _____

2. Mrs. Ezra was talking to Dr. Du in the Sub-basement floor when she went up three floors. Which meeting was she going to? _____

   Give the number of the sentence that provides the best evidence for your answer. _____ Complete this equation to show what the elevator did: -2 + 3 = _____

3. Mr. Keyes is on the third floor and he goes down five floors to his meeting. What meeting is he going to? _____

   Give the number of the sentence that provides the best evidence for your answer. _____

   Complete this equation to show what the elevator did: 3 + –5 = _____

4. Mr. Garcia enters the building on the main floor. He goes down two floors and remembers that he has a meeting about how much money the company is making. On what floor is his meeting? _____ How many floors does he have to go up now?_____

   Write an equation to show what the elevator did: _____

5. Mrs. Singer is on the fourth floor and she has to go down five floors. What meeting is she attending? _____

   Write an equation to show what the elevator did: _____

6. Ms. Long is on the storage floor, and she remembers it's time to go to the meeting to receive her award. She takes the elevator and goes up 7 floors. What meeting is she attending? _____

   Give the number of the sentence that provides the best evidence for your answer. _____

   Write an equation to show what the elevator did: _____

7. Who is the president of the company? _____ Question 6 and sentence _____ provide the best evidence for your answer.

40—The Function Machines Go Nuts!

[1]In the function machine room, the machines are not working right and no one can figure out why! [2]When a function machine works right, it takes every number that is put in and does the same operation (+, −, x ,÷) to each one before it spits it out. [3]Here is an example of a function machine in good working order.

This first machine was programmed to multiply each number in the In column by the same number. The answer is in the Out column.

In	Out
11	33
12	36
13	39
14	42
15	45

Questions

1. Figure out what number it is multiplying by. Use complete sentences to explain your thinking.

_____

_____

Now, the machines below have gone nuts! There is <u>one</u> mistake in each one. You've been hired as a math detective. For each table shown, answer the questions below. If you fix the machines, you will get a math certificate that will hang in the functions room Hall of Fame.

2. a. What is this machine supposed to be doing? Use complete sentences to explain your thinking.

_____

_____

In	Out
0	5
1	6
2	7
3	11
4	9

b. What did it do wrong? Use complete sentences to explain your thinking.

_____

_____

c. What number in the Out column should you replace to fix the machine? _____ What number would you replace it with? _____

3. a. What is this machine supposed to be doing? Use complete sentences to explain your thinking.

In	Out
48	7
42	7
12	2
30	5
6	1

_____

_____

b. What did it do wrong? Use complete sentences to explain your thinking.

_____

_____

c. What number should go in the Out column to fix the machine? _____

4. a. What is this machine supposed to be doing? Use complete sentences to explain your thinking.

In	Out
1000	100
100	10
10	1
1	10
40	4

_____

_____

b. What did it do wrong? Use complete sentences to explain your thinking.

_____

_____

c. What number should go in the Out column to fix the machine? _____

5. a. What is the machine supposed to be doing? Use complete sentences to explain your thinking.

In	Out
1	4
0	3
-1	2
-2	5
-3	0

_____

_____

b. What did it do wrong? Use complete sentences to explain your thinking.

_____

_____

c. What number should go in the Out column to fix the machine? _____

ANSWERS

Answers show correct student responses to the questions, though wording may vary. Accept responses with the the same meaning. You may use the Rubric described on page viii for scoring activities.

NOTE: Parentheses are used to show extra explanations not required of the student, coordinates or order of operations.

I. NUMBER & NUMERATION

1—The Train Ride, p. 2

1. 1, 2, 4, 5, 10, and 20. Sentence 12.

2. Mrs. Winterbloom, Mrs. Applecrumb, and Ms. Twinkle. Their seat numbers are 5, 10, and 20, which are factors of 20.

3. No. Mr. Lyons is in seat 19, and 19 is not a factor of 20. (19 goes into 20 once with remainder 1.)

4. a. Sentence 15.

5. Mr. Papas and Ms. Kamen. (Mr. Papas is in seat 6 and Ms. Kamen is in seat 27. 6 and 27 are multiples of 3. 3 is a factor of both 6 and 27.)

6. One is a factor of every number because 1 goes into any number OR Every number is divisible by 1.

7. d. (Everyone on the train should get a ride because every number is a multiple of 1, or 1 is a factor of every number.)

2—Who's Who, p. 4

1. 1. Any number times 1 is itself.

2. 2. The tree is 1, so each flower must be 2.

3. 0. The tree is 1, so the butterfly must be 0, since any number times 0 is 0.

4. c. (Since the flower is 2, the leaf must be 3.)

5. b.

6. The number 1 is called the identity for multiplication because any number times 1 is itself.

3—Well Rounded, p. 6

1. 4,731. Mary's number must be 4,731 because when you add up the digits, you get 15, and 3 goes into 15 evenly, so 3 also goes into 4,731 evenly. Sentences 4 and 6.

2. a. 4,915.
   b. $4,915 \div 3 = 1,638$ R1; $4 + 9 + 1 + 5 = 19$. (When you divide by 3, Luis's number gives a remainder. Also, if you add the digits of Luis's number you get 19, and 3 does not go into 19 evenly.)

3. 1,577. $\frac{1}{3} \times 4,731 = 1,577$. (Daycia's number is one-third of Mary's number.) Sentence 7.

4. 9,646. $4,731 + 4,915 = 9,646$ (Joey's number is the sum of Mary's number and Luis's number.) Sentence 8.

5. When you divide 1,577 by 3, you get 525 R2. When you divide 9,646 by 3, you get 3,215 R1 OR (by using the divisibility rule for 3): Adding the digits of 1,577 you get 20, and 3 doesn't go into 20 evenly, so Daycia's number is not divisible by 3. Adding the digits of 9,646, you get 25, and 3 doesn't go into 25 evenly, so Joey's number is not divisible by 3 either.

6. Yes. Joey's number ends in 6, so it's an even number. All even numbers are divisible by 2. Luis's number is divisible by 5 because all numbers that end in 0 or 5 are divisible by 5.

7. 10,000. (Joey's number, 9,646, rounded to the nearest thousand)
   2,000. (Daycia's number, 1,577, rounded to the nearest thousand)

4—The Inca Quipu, p. 8

1. 160 years. 1560 – 1400. Sentence 1.

2. No. Multiplying and dividing are ways of calculating, and the quipu was not used as a calculator. Sentence 17.

3. b. Sentence 12.

4. $(4 \times 1,000) + (2 \times 100) + (3 \times 10) + (1 \times 1)$ OR

   $(4 \times 10^3) + (2 \times 10^2) + (3 \times 10^1) + (1 \times 1)$.

5. 8,035.

6. 17. If you have two place values, the smallest number you can make is 17 because you can put seven knots in the ones place and one knot in the tens place OR with two place values, you must have at least one ten; that leaves seven ones.

7.

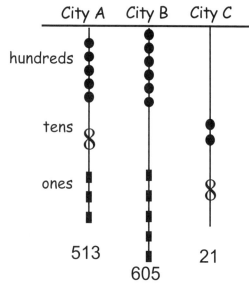

```
        City A   City B   City C
hundreds
tens
ones

        513               21
            605
```

5—At the Arcade, p. 11

1. 3 coins. Sentence 2. 15 cents.

2. 16p

   1d 6p   p = pennies
   (2n 6p)   n = nickels
   3n 1p   d = dimes
   1d 1n 1p

3. (8p)
   1n 3p

4. Mark has nickels (2) and pennies (6) and Luis has pennies (8), since Mark

and Luis have the same amount of coins.

5. No. If one person has twice as much money, it does not mean that the person has twice as many coins. Coins have different values.

6. 2 games. The machine takes only nickels. Mark has 2 nickels and Luis has none, so they can play 2 games.

7. 25p   1q
   5n   1d 3n
   1d 2n 5p   2n 15p
   2d 5p   1d 15p
   3n 10p   2d 1n
   4n 5p   (1n 1d 10p)
   1n 20p

8. Sentence 10. She had a nickel (1), dime (1) and pennies (10). (She had 12 coins that add to 25 cents.)

9. One. She had only one nickel.

6—The Sieve of Eratosthenes, p. 13

(On the chart, the prime numbers should be circled. They are as follows:) 2, 3, 5, 7, 11, 13, 17, 19, 23, 29, 31, 37, 41, 43, 47, 53, 59, 61, 67, 71, 73, 79, 83, 89, and 97.

1. 82. 276 – 194 = 82. Sentences 3 and 4.

2. A composite number is any number after 1 that has factors other than 1 and itself.

3. d.

4. All the multiples of 5 end with 5 or 0.

5. The multiples of 11 are found along the same diagonal: 11, 22, 33, etc., OR they have the same two digits on the table. (This last fact is true only for multiples of 11 less than 100.) You can tell by drawing a line diagonally down to the right, starting at 11.

6. The number 200 is not prime because it has many factors. (We can see that it is divisible by 2, for example.)

7—Miguel's Memory Games, p. 15

1. 11 years old. Sentence 5.
2. Emily. Sentence 4.
3. a. E, 11, G, 15, I, 19, K, 23, M, 27, O, 31

   b. Miguel. Miguel lost because he should have skipped 29 and said 31 after 27.
4. 2. Sentence 11.
5. A prime number is any number after 1 with only two factors, 1 and itself.
6. A composite number is a number after 1 that has more than 2 different factors.
7. a. 2, 3, 5, 7, 11, 13, 17, 19, 23, 29, 31, 37, 41, 43, 47, 53, 59.

   b. Miguel. He made a mistake because 51 is not prime. The number 51 is divisible by 3 and 17.
8. Both 57 and 111 are divisible by 3, so they are not prime.

8—A Walk Through the Park, p. 17

1. Sentences 3 and 4.

2. Second generation: 4
   Third generation: 8
   Fourth generation: 16
3. 30.   2 + 4 + 8 + 16
4. Yes. Pepin is incorrect because each branch makes two branches, so you have to multiply and not add.
5. Sentence 13. Base.
6. Sentence 15. Exponent OR Power.
7. The exponent tells you how many times to multiply the base times itself. Sentence 16.
8. Two to the fifth power. Sentence 14.
9. No. Sentence 17.

10. $2^3, 3^2, 5^2, 2^5, 6^2, 9^2$
    $2 \times 2 \times 2 = 8$
    $3 \times 3 = 9$
    $5 \times 5 = 25$
    $2 \times 2 \times 2 \times 2 \times 2 = 32$
    $6 \times 6 = 36$
    $9 \times 9 = 81.$

9—Mrs. Sanchez's Four Children, p. 20

1.

Name	How often: every...	1	2	3	4	5	6	7	8	9	10	11	12	13	14	15	16	17	18	19	20	21	22	23	24	25	26	27	28	29	30
Maria	vacuum 2 days		X		X		X		X		X		X		X		X		X		X		X		X		X		X		X
Luis	laundry 3 days			X			X			X			X			X			X			X			X			X			X
Juan	bathe 5 days					X					X					X					X					X					X
Vero	windows 15 days															X															X

2. $15. $1.50 x 10. Sentences 7 and 12 (on the chart).
3. Every 6 days. (Five times that month.)
4. Every 10 days. (Three times that month.)
5. Once every 30 days.
6. 30. Multiples of 2: 2, 4, 6, 8, 10, 12, 14, 16, 18, 20, 22, 24, 26, 28, <u>30</u>...
   Multiples of 3: 3, 6, 9, 12, 15, 18, 21, 24, 27, <u>30</u>...
   Multiples of 5: 5, 10, 15, 20, 25, <u>30</u>...
   Multiples of 15: 15, <u>30</u>...
7. Maria. She vacuumed 15 times and made $2 each time.
   Maria $30.   15 x $2.00
   Luis $15.   10 x $1.50
   Juan $18.   6 x $3.00
   Veronica $20.   2 x $10.00

II. OPERATIONS

10—Off to the Movies!, p. 24

1. $15.00. 3 x $5.00. Sentences 1 and 2.
2. $36.50. $16 + $14 + $6.50
3. $ 7.00. $3.50 + $2 + $1.50. Sentence 7.
4. $24.00. $15 + $7 + $2
5. $12.50. $36.50 – $24
6. Small. There was $12.50 left and Amy bought the $4.50 medium popcorn.

Then there was $8 left, so they each bought a small popcorn at $4 each.

7. No. They would still have been short $1. Adding $3 to what they had before they bought the two small popcorns would have given them $11. Two extra large popcorns cost $12.

11—The Parking Lot Problem, p. 26

1.

	A	B
1st hour	8.00	6.00
2nd hour	+ 1.20	+ 2.50
3rd hour	+ 1.20	+ 2.50
$\frac{1}{2}$ hour	+ 0.60	+ 1.25
Total	$11.00	$12.25

2. Parking Lot A. Parking Lot A costs $11 and Parking Lot B costs $ 12.25.

3. Parking Lot B. $14.50. It would be cheaper to pay the maximum rate. Since 7 hours would reach the maximum rate at both lots, B would cost $14.50, and A would cost $15.

4. (Answers may vary.) Parking lots charge more for the first hour because this way they can get more money from people that need to park for an hour or less.

12—The Potato Race, p. 28

1. 3 minutes 40 seconds. 3 minutes 75 seconds (Emily's time) – 35 seconds = 3 minutes 40 seconds. (Change 4 minutes 15 seconds to 3 minutes 75 seconds.) Sentence 14.

2. 4 minutes 30 seconds. 3 minutes 40 seconds (Amanda's time) + 50 seconds = 4 minutes 30 seconds. Sentence 15.

3. a. (Amanda's time was least, at 3 minutes 40 seconds.)

4. 6 minutes 40 seconds. 8 minutes (Eddy's time) – 1 minute 20 seconds (Ramon's time) = 6 minutes 40 seconds.

5. Mrs. Sanchez said that no part of the body was allowed to touch the potato. Sentence 7.

13—The Camping Trails, p. 30

1. 2.4 miles. 1.4 + 1 = 2.4. (Trail 3 is 1.4 miles and Trail 2 is 1 mile.)

2. .7 miles. 2.3 – 1.6 = .7 (All of Trail 1 minus Lake Agua Clara's distance from the entrance.)

3. 10,560 feet. 5,280 (feet) x 2 (miles) = 10,560. Sentence 7.

4. 2.9 miles. 1 + 1.4 + .5 = 2.9.

5. It is closer to go back by way of the waterfall. .7 + 1 + 1.4 = 3.1 is less than 1.6 + 2 = 3.6. (Lake Agua Clara to the waterfall is .7 of a mile, Trail 2 is 1 mile, and Trail 3 is 1.4 mile; Lake Agua Clara to the entrance is 1.6 miles, and Road 2 is 2 miles.)

14—The Mystery Fraction, p. 32

1. c.

2. Fraction A is bigger. $\frac{3}{4}$ is the same as $\frac{6}{8}$, so $\frac{7}{8}$ is bigger than $\frac{3}{4}$.

3. Neither. Both are equal. $\frac{3}{4} = \frac{6}{8}$.

4. $1\frac{5}{8}$. $\frac{7}{8} + \frac{3}{4} = 1\frac{5}{8}$. ($\frac{3}{4} = \frac{6}{8}$; $\frac{13}{8} = 1\frac{5}{8}$)

5.

6. (Accept any fraction between 1 and $1\frac{5}{8}$.) I chose this as Fraction X because it is bigger than 1 but smaller than $1\frac{5}{8}$. (Answers will vary. $1\frac{1}{4}$ is one example of a fraction that is between 1 and $1\frac{5}{8}$.)

7. (Accept any fraction between the student's Fraction X, from question 6, and $1\frac{5}{8}$.) I found it by adding the two fractions, $1\frac{5}{8}$ and [X], and then dividing by two [which gives a fraction halfway between] OR I looked for a fraction bigger than [X] but smaller than $1\frac{5}{8}$. (Answers will vary.)

15—The Rainy Week, p. 34

1. City A: $3\frac{5}{8}$ ": $2 + 1 + \frac{1}{4} + \frac{1}{4} + \frac{1}{8} = 3 + \frac{4}{8} + \frac{1}{8}$
   City B: $9\frac{3}{4}$ ": $4 + 1\frac{1}{4} + 1\frac{1}{2} + 1\frac{3}{4} + 1 + \frac{1}{4} = 8 + \frac{5}{4} + \frac{2}{4} = 8\frac{7}{4}$

2. The chart says it did not rain every day. The weather station predicted it would, but the chart shows three 0s for rainfall amounts.

3. b. Sentence 8.

4. Sunday.

5. $\frac{7}{8}$ " more. 1" – $\frac{1}{8}$ ".

6. No. Sentence 6. City A got $3\frac{5}{8}$ " of rain and flooding was supposed to happen if they got more than 6".

7. a. Yes. Sentence 7. City B got $9\frac{3}{4}$ " of rain and flooding was supposed to happen if they got more than 8".
   b. $1\frac{3}{4}$ ". $9\frac{3}{4}$ " – 8". (City B got more.)

8. City B. Sentence 4.

9. $1\frac{3}{4}$ ". 2" – $\frac{1}{4}$ ".

16—The Best Pancake Recipe, p. 36

1. Sentence 1. 11 friends.

2. 3. Sentence 12.

3. 36 pancakes. (12 people x 3 = 36 pancakes)

4. Olga should multiply this recipe by 4.

5. 4c flour, 4c buttermilk (or 1 quart), $5\frac{1}{3}$ T sugar, 4t baking powder, 2t baking soda, 2t salt, 4T vegetable oil, 4 eggs.

6. $\frac{1}{3}$ of a dozen.

7. 1 quart. Sentence 14.

8. $1\frac{1}{3}$. Sentence 13.

9. No. She was supposed to combine the dry ingredients first and then the wet ingredients next. Sentences 4 and 5.

10. She turned the pancake too soon. Sentence 10.

17—The 2002 State Shopping Spree, p. 38

1. Neither. Both states have the same tax. Facts 2 and 7.

2. $20 ($250 x .08).

3. c. Facts 7 and 13.

4. It's the same ($299.25) in either state. In North Dakota: $285 x .05 = $14.25, and $285 + $14.25 = $299.25. It doesn't matter which state I buy it in, since Oregon has no sales tax.

5. Virginia: $800. $20,000 x .04.
   Florida: $1,400. $20,000 x .07.
   Delaware: no tax.

6. Delaware: $20,000.
   $20,000 + (0 x $20,000)
   Virginia: $20,800.
   $20,000 + (.04 x $20,000)
   Florida: $21,400.
   $20,000 + (.07 x $20,000)

7. No. It depends on the original price of each item.

8. Neither. $5.00 + $9.00 + $12.00 = $26.00. $26.00 x .05 = $1.56. $5.00 x .06 = .30. $9.00 x .06 = .54. $12.00 x .06 = .72. (Add:) .30 + .54 + .72 = $1.56. Adding the items first, I get $26.00, and the tax on that is $1.56. Finding the tax on each item first, I get a tax of .30 for the $5 umbrella, .54 for the suntan lotion, and .72 for the beach towel. Adding the taxes separately also gives a total tax of $1.56.

III. GEOMETRY

18—Angle Billboards, p. 42

1. 25°. ∠ABF is 90°, and since ∠ABC is 40° then ∠CBF is 50°. Since ∠CBE and ∠EBF are congruent, each angle is 25°.

2. 60°. Take 180° and subtract 120°. (∠TED is 90°. 90° + 30 ° = 120°, which leaves 60° for ∠TER.)

3. d. (Since ∠DXR is 20° and ∠AXB is congruent to it, ∠ABX is also 20°. 180° minus 40° is 140°, so ∠AXD is 140°.)

4. c. (Since ∠RXE is 90°, 90° minus the measure of ∠DXE, which is 80°, gives 10° for ∠RXD. Adding the measure of ∠AXR, which is 90°, to the measure of

∠RXD gives 100° for the measure of ∠AXD.)

19—Trip to the Game, p. 44

1. b. Sentence 8.
2. 57,600 square feet. 360 x 160 = 57,600
3. 4,700 square feet. 94 x 50 = 4,700
4. 52,900 square feet. 57,600 – 4,700 = 52,900
5. 120 yards. 360 ÷ 3 = 120
6. 360 feet. 120 + 120 = 240; 60 + 60 = 120; 240 + 120 = 360. Sentence 21.
7. About 12 (mathematically) or 10 (actual courts). Divide the area of a football field by the area of a basketball court. 57,600 ÷ 4,700 is about 12.3. Alternate answer 10: Only 10 actual courts can fit inside the football field. There is extra space around the edges of the field, but it isn't in the right shape to be used as basketball courts.

20—The Perennial Garden, p. 46

1. No. (The garden must be rectangular.) Sentence 4.
2. Sentences 2 and 4. Perimeter is the distance around the outside of a shape.
3. No. Sentence 7.
4. a. Sentences 5 and 6.
5. (To be considered completely correct, grid drawings must include all of the dimensions listed in Column a, below. Column b shows area.)

a	b
1' x 11'	11' sq ft
2' x 10'	20' sq ft
3' x 9'	27' sq ft
4' x 8'	32' sq ft
5' x 7'	35' sq ft
6' x 6' (Ami's design)	36

6. 6' x 6'. 36 sq ft Sentence 8.
7. 2' x 10'. 20 sq ft Sentence 12.
8. Disagree. Ami's garden has an area of 36 sq ft and Miguel's garden has an area of 20 sq ft.

9. (Answers may vary.) I agree with Miguel because Ami's garden is in the shape of a square so it would be harder to reach the center of the garden to weed unless there was a path to get to the center.

21—The Quadrilateral Factory, p. 48

Answers to The Quadrilateral Family Picture: A—quadrilateral, B—parallelogram, C—trapezoid, D—rectangle, E—rhombus, F—square

1. a and b. (A polygon is a closed, many-sided shape.) Sentence 35.
2. A parallelogram is a 4-sided shape or quadrilateral with opposite sides parallel. (Accept any picture fitting the above description.) Sentence 6.
3. A trapezoid is a quadrilateral with only two sides parallel. (Accept any picture fitting the above description.) Sentence 8.
4. Yes. A rectangle is a parallelogram because it has opposite sides parallel. Sentences 21 and 22.
5. It is both. A square has equal sides, which makes it a rhombus, and four right angles, which makes it a rectangle. Sentence 32.
6. A trapezoid is not a parallelogram because a parallelogram has two pairs of opposite parallel sides, and a trapezoid has only one pair of parallel opposite sides.

22—The Toy Box Project, p. 52

1. Boxes A and B are each 9 cubic feet in volume. $4 \times 1\frac{1}{2} \times 1\frac{1}{2} = 9$ and $3 \times 1\frac{1}{2} \times 2 = 9$.
2. No, both boxes have the same volume.
3. 36" = 3 feet, and 18" = $1\frac{1}{2}$ feet.
4. $6\frac{3}{4}$ cubic feet. $3 \times 1\frac{1}{2} \times 1\frac{1}{2} = 6\frac{3}{4}$
5. No. Box C has less volume than either Box A or Box B.
6. He would save about $37.00. $237 – $200 = $37. Sentences 4 and 6.

7. Purple. Sentence 9.

8. Box A. Since the doll is $3\frac{1}{2}$ feet long and has to lie flat, Box A would be long enough.

9. $1\frac{3}{4}$ feet. $14 \div 4 = 3\frac{1}{2}$; $3\frac{1}{2} \div 2 = 1\frac{3}{4}$. (The volume 14 cubic feet is divided by 4 and then by 2.)

23—The Case of the Missing Money, p. 54

1. (Answers include all elements on the grid below except the X, which belongs to question 2.)

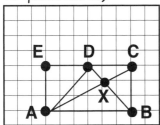

2. (7,3). (See location of X in grid above.)

3. Rectangle. It has 4 sides and 4 right angles.

4. 6 units. 3 units.

5. 18 square units. I multiplied length times width OR I multiplied base times height OR I counted the squares inside the shape.

6. They are both triangles because they have three sides.

7. 9 square units. ABCE is a rectangle. You can get the answer by finding half of the rectangle area ($\frac{1}{2} \times 18 = 9$) OR You can use the area of a triangle formula, which is one half of base (6) x height (3).

8. The height and the base are both the same. The height is 3 and the base is 6.

9. Both triangles have the same base and the same height.

10. 6 square units. 9 – 3 = 6. (Area can be found as in question 7.)

11. 18, 9, 6.
    Sentence 11 (18 = area of ABCE).

Sentence 12 (9 = area of ABC).
Sentence 13 (6 = area of ABD – 3).

24—The Math Teachers' Room, p. 56

1. b. (10 x 4.) Sentences 6 and 14.

2. 24 square feet. 8 x 6 = 48 and 48 ÷ 2 = 24.

3. d. (Multiply 6 x 6 = 36. She is sitting on the square sofa.)

4. 28.26 square feet. 3 x 3 x 3.14.

5. d.

6. 16 feet. We know the rectangle sofa is 10 feet long, so one wall is 22 feet long. (6 + 10 + 6). Since the room is a square, the wall with a window is also 22 feet long, so the window must be 22 – 6 feet (square sofa), or 16 feet long.

7. 484 square feet. Since the room is a square, I multiplied 22 x 22. Sentence 7.

IV. PROBABILITY

25—Sum of Six, p. 60

1. c.

2. 2, 11, and 12. The only way to get 2 is 1 + 1. The only way to get 11 is 5 + 6 or 6 + 5. The only way to get 12 is 6 + 6.

3. Sum of 7: 1 + 6, 6 + 1, 5 + 2, 2 + 5, 3 + 4, and 4 + 3. Sum of 8: 2 + 6, 6 + 2, 3 + 5, 5 + 3, and 4 + 4.

4. There are more ways of getting those sums than other sums.

5. d. [The 36 ways include the following: (1,1), (1,2), (1,3), (1,4), (1,5), (1,6), (2,1), (2,2), (2,3), (2,4), (2,5), (2,6), (3,1), (3,2), etc.]

6. a. (Answers vary. Chart and answer should indicate that middle numbers were rolled the greatest number of times.)
   b. (Answers vary.)

26—The Buttons, p. 62

1. 12. Sentence 4.

2. 3. Sentence 4.

3. 29. (12 red + 8 blue + 6 yellow + 3 purple)

4. c. (She has 12 chances out of 29.)

5. b. (She has 3 chances out of 29.)

6. If Veni gave the first red button to her mom, then the jar has 28 buttons left. Of those only 11 are red now. The chances that she will pick another red button are 11 out of 28.

27—The Spinner Game, p. 64

1. He gets 2 points. Sentence 4.

2. She loses 1 point. Sentence 3.

3. She gets 2 points. Zero is even. $\frac{0}{2}$ = 0. Sentence 6.

4. –1. 3 x 2 pts. = 6 pts. 7 x –1 pt. = –7 pts. 6 pts. – 7 pts. = –1 pt. (There are three odd numbers and seven even numbers.)

5. 2. 4 x 2 pts. = 8 pts. 6 x –1 pts. = –6 pts. 8 – 6 pts. = 2 pts. (There are four even numbers and six odd numbers.)

6. $\frac{1}{2}$

7. $\frac{1}{2}$

8. $\frac{1}{2}$

9. $\frac{1}{2}$

10. Yes. The odds of winning were the same for each player.

11. Sentence 9. 3 points.

12. Sentence 10. 3 points.

13. You can take 9 and try first to divide by 2, 3, 4, 5, and so on. You find that 9 has more than two factors (1 and itself) because 3 goes into it evenly.

14. If 51 were prime, Juan would have more chances of winning because there would be more prime numbers than composite numbers on the spinner.

15. He probably showed Daria that 51 is divisible by 3, since he wanted to convince her that 51 was not prime. (Divisible means it can be divided without a remainder.)

16. Daria. 4 x 3 = 12. (Daria got four composite numbers, 9, 4, 4, and 51.) 2 x 3 = 6 points (Juan got two prime numbers, 2 and 11.)

28—The Game of Dish, p. 68

1. a. Sentence 9.

2. A player can reach 6 by getting 1 point six times OR 5 points and then 1 point OR 1 point and then 5 points. (Accept any two ways.)

3. 1st turn: 0, 2nd turn: 0, 3rd turn: 0, 4th turn: 1. Final score: 1.

4. It's very hard to get all six stones all with the same color, so that's why a player would get so many more points. Most of the time a player got no points. (Answers will vary.)

29—The Breakfast Special, p. 71

1. Pancakes with bacon or waffles with bacon. Sentence 5.

2. $\frac{1}{2}$ She has two choices of possible meals, so waffles and bacon is one of her total choices.

3. Scrambled eggs with toast and bacon, or pancakes with bacon, or waffles with bacon. Sentence 6.

4. a. Scrambled eggs with toast and bacon, or scrambled eggs with toast and sausage, or pancakes and sausage, or pancakes and bacon, or waffles and bacon, or waffles and sausage.

   b. 6

5. $\frac{1}{6}$

6. Yes. (Answers will vary. Accept an answer in which all members eat a different meal. e.g., Josie: pancakes and bacon. Hector: waffles and sausage. Grandma: waffles and bacon. Mrs. Cavallo: eggs with toast and bacon. Mr. Cavallo: eggs with toast and sausage.)

7. No. There are only six different meals that can be created.

V. STATISTICS

30—The Great Goldfish Giveaway, p. 74

1. 36. (18 x 2) Sentence 1. (The second dot on the graph, indicating 18 people, should be circled.)

2. d. (30 + 36 + 40 = 106; 28 + 30 + 10 + 2 + 8 = 78; 106 – 78 = 28)

3. 184. 30 + 36 + 40 +28 +30 + 10 + 2 + 8.

4. Yes. A total of 184 goldfish were given away and the owner had 200.

5. c.

6. The number of customers kept going up from 9 A.m. to 11 A.m. (Also, she gave away more than half the fish in the first three hours, and there were still seven hours left.)

7. A popular restaurant was having a lunch special, so maybe people went next door to eat. Sentence 5.

31—Jameel's Math Scores, p. 76

1. It represents the percent score Jameel got on his math tests.

2. It represents the different tests.

3. 75. Sentence 2. (All his scores are multiples of 5.)

4. 75, 65, 80, 85, and 90.

5. 79. (75 + 65 + 80 + 85 + 90) ÷ 5. Sentence 4.

6. No. Jameel's scores might be going up but that does not mean his next score will be better. (Tests 3, 4, and 5 do show increases, but there is no guarantee the next score will continue the trend.)

7. 80. (75 + 65 + 80 + 85 + 90 + 85) ÷ 6.

8. One point.

9. 97. 80 x 6 = 480. 480 – 70 – 80 – 68 – 80 – 85 = 97. ([70 + 80 + 68 + 80 + 85 + ?] ÷ 6 = 80, so multiply 80 x 6 and subtract all the numbers to find the missing test score.)

10. (Graph should include labels for title [e.g., "Amanda's Test Scores"] and axes [e.g., "Tests" for x axis and "Percent" for y axis] and properly show these scores: 70, 80, 68, 80, 85, 97.)

32—Cody's Homework Graph, p. 80

1.

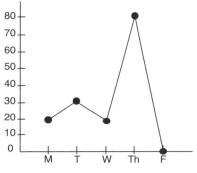

2. Tuesday. Sentence 3.

3. Thursday. Sentences 4 and 5.

4. 20 minutes. Cody spent the same amount of time two days reading his social studies book. The only two days that show the same amount of time spent on homework are Monday and Wednesday. On each of those days, he spent 20 minutes on homework.

5. 50 minutes. 80 – 30 = 50.

6. No. Cody spent a total of 150 minutes on homework. His dad promised him a little gift if he spent at least three hours (or 180 minutes) on homework. Sentence 2.

33—Temperature Tale of Two Cities, p. 82

1.
Boston		Miami	
8 a.m.	40°	8 a.m.	55°
9 a.m.	45°	9 a.m.	60°
10 a.m.	55°	10 a.m.	55°
11 a.m.	40°	11 a.m.	60°
12 Noon	35°	12 Noon	65°
1 p.m.	30°	1 p.m.	60°

2. 15°. 55° – 40° = 15°.

3. Boston. It went up 10° from 9 a.m. to 10 a.m.

4. 10 a.m. They both had the same temperature because the exact same dot on the graph is used to show both.

5. From 12 p.m. (noon) to 1 p.m., the temperature was dropping in both cities.

6. 59°. (55 + 60 + 55 + 60 + 65 + 60) ÷ 6 = 355 ÷ 6 = 59.167.

7. 41°. (40 + 45 + 55 + 40 + 35 + 30) ÷ 6 = 245 ÷ 6 = 40.833.

34—Making Money Mowing, p. 84

1. Movies, Gift, T-shirt, Video Game, and Money Saved. (In that order.)

2. $10. Sentence 2. $\frac{1}{10}$ × 100 = 10.

3. $20. Sentence 3. $\frac{1}{5}$ × $100 = 20.

4. The T-shirt and the Video Game look like they take about half of the circle. Half of the circle is $50. (If students answer "savings and gift," commend their thinking, but explain that savings is not considered an expense.)

5. $63. Gift $10 + T-shirt $20 + Movies $8 + Video game $25.

6. $37. 100 – 63 = 37. Sentence 6.

7. 10%. $\frac{1}{10}$ = 10/100 (which is 10%).

8. 63%. $63 out of $100 = $\frac{63}{100}$ (which is 63%).

9. d.

10. 36 degrees. (sentence 2 says she spent $\frac{1}{10}$ on her grandfather's gift; one tenth of 360 is 36.)

35—The World Record Fish Report, p. 87

1. 2,196 lbs. 2,664 – 468.

2. c. Bluefin tunas are not the biggest animals in the ocean. In the chart, the Great White Shark is a lot bigger.

3. 1,269 oz. (79 × 16) + 5

4. Chart Answers:

Row 1: (Blue), 454 lbs. (sentence 15), Martha's Vineyard, MA, 1996, (sentence 16).

Row 2: Hammerhead, 991 lbs. (2,664–1,673, sentence 22), Sarasota, FL (sentence 23), (1982).

Row 3: Shortfin Mako, 1,115 lbs. (454 × 3 – 247, sentences 27, 29, 15), (Black River, Mauritius), 1988 (sentence 23).

Row 4: Tiger, (1,780 lbs.), So. Carolina (sentence 24), 1964 (1959 + 5 years, sentence 26).

Row 5: (Great White), 2,664 lbs. (454 + 2,210, sentences 15, 18, 19), Australia, 1959 (sentence 20).

VI. PRE-ALGEBRA

36—The King Orders the Operations!, p. 92

1. a.

2. The rules were necessary because too many people were getting the wrong answer and there was a lot of confusion. Sentences 4 and 5.

3. No. Sentence 12.

4. No. Sentence 13. (You do whichever one is first from left to right.)

5. c.

6. 33. Sentence 15. You do the work in parentheses first then work the problem from left to right. (In this case, use addition then division then multiplication.)

37—Symbol Says…, p. 94

1. Eddy: 1; 4 × $\frac{1}{4}$
   Luis: $\frac{1}{12}$; $\frac{1}{3}$ × $\frac{1}{4}$

2. Eddy: 16; 4 ÷ $\frac{1}{4}$
   Luis: $\frac{4}{3}$ OR 1$\frac{1}{3}$; $\frac{1}{3}$ ÷ $\frac{1}{4}$

3. Eddy: 3$\frac{3}{4}$; 4 – $\frac{1}{4}$
   Amanda: $\frac{1}{4}$; $\frac{1}{2}$ – $\frac{1}{4}$

4. Eddy: 4$\frac{1}{4}$; 4 + $\frac{1}{4}$
   Luis: $\frac{7}{12}$; $\frac{1}{3}$ + $\frac{1}{4}$

5. STAR: $\frac{1}{4}$; $1 \times \frac{1}{4}$
   PLANET: 4 ; $1 \div \frac{1}{4}$
   COMET: $\frac{3}{4}$; $1 - \frac{1}{4}$
   SUN: $1\frac{1}{4}$; $1 + \frac{1}{4}$

6. 0. When 0 is divided by $\frac{1}{4}$, you get 0.

38—The Case of the Missing Numbers, p. 96

1. 6, 7, 8, 9, 10, 20.
2. 5 + 5 is not greater than 10.
3. 5, 6, 7, 8, 9.
4. Ten cannot be used because 10 – 5 is not less than 5.
5. 6, 7, 8, 9.
6. Yes. If you add 6 $\frac{1}{2}$ + 5 you get 11 $^1/_2$, which is greater than 10.
7. Yes. The sum of 48 + 5 is greater than 10.
8. An open circle means that you cannot use that number because it does not make the inequality true. Sentence 5.
9. It means that all the numbers that follow the arrowhead also make the inequality true.
10.

10

11. The numbers that make both inequalities true are between 5 and 10 (not including 5 and 10).

39—The Busy Elevator, p. 98

1. Lunch meeting. Sentence 10.
   2. (–2 + 4 = 2)
2. The meeting to create more TV ads. Sentence 9. 1. (–2 + 3 = 1)

3. A meeting about a new product. Sentence 8. –2. (3 + –5 = –2)
4. Floor 3. 5. 0 + (–2) + 5 = 3.
5. A computer meeting. 4 + (–5) = –1.
6. The awards meeting. Sentence 12. –3 + 7 = 4.
7. Ms. Long. Sentence 12.

40—The Function Machines Go Nuts!, p. 100

1. It's multiplying every number in the In column by 3. The answers are in the Out column (e.g., you can divide 33 by 11 to get 3).
2. a. It's supposed to be adding 5 each time.
   b. When 3 went in, it added 8 instead of 5.
   c. 11. 8. (Replace the 11 in the Out column with an 8.)
3. a. It's supposed to be dividing by 6.
   b. It got the wrong number when dividing 48 by 6.
   c. 8.
4. a. It's supposed to be dividing by 10.
   b. It got the wrong number when dividing 1 by 10.
   c. $\frac{1}{10}$ OR .1 . (Change the second 10 to $\frac{1}{10}$ or .1 .)
5. a. It's supposed to be adding three each time.
   b. It got the wrong number when adding –2 + 3 OR it added 7 instead of 3. (It should have added 3 to get 1 instead of 5.)
   c. 1. (Replace the 5 in the Out column.)

Teacher Notes